DOUBLE SALES / ZERO SALESPEOPLE

Optimize Your Sales And Marketing Into One Business Development Strategy That Works!

By Andy Buyting
&
Jessica Embree

TulipMediaGroup.com

◆◆◆

Contents

Preface

By Andy Buyting

SMarketing, by definition, is the integration of sales and marketing into a single business development strategy. That's how we define SMarketing at Tulip Media Group.

In most traditional companies, sales and marketing are two separate initiatives, or strategies, which we feel hinder a company's growth potential. The way we see it, when these two departments don't work seamlessly together, companies struggle to grow. Separating sales and marketing into two silos, as is traditionally done, significantly restricts your ability to drive real sales.

In most traditional companies, marketing is charged with going out and finding qualified leads. They do this through branding, marketing, website development, social media advertising, and other more direct forms of lead generation. Essentially, they go out into the world to get the attention of the target audience interested in the products and services their company is selling. Once they have an interested party, marketing will typically throw that lead over to the sales department. Sales is then charged with taking that qualified lead and bringing them down through the sales funnel to a successful close.

The challenge with this approach is that marketing and sales are working independently instead of cohesively. Each department is often incentivized with different goals. The goal of marketing is to find qualified leads, not necessarily closed sales, and it's most often incented to do just that. Marketing departments are bonused on hitting their "qualified leads" metrics, regardless of whether those leads close or not. Sales, on the other hand, has a goal to close more business, regardless of where the leads come from. The challenge here is that when the business does not grow, marketing is very quick to blame sales for not closing the qualified leads they've provided while sales blames marketing for sending over poorly qualified leads or not enough leads. This can result in limited cohesiveness for the overall business development approach and certainly many missed opportunities.

To be really effective, there needs to be elements of sales in your marketing efforts and elements of marketing in your sales efforts. The sales component of the marketing message should cue your prospects and prepare them for the sales journey they are about to take. To be effective in marketing, you need to have that sales mind-set from the very beginning. Conversely, to be effective in sales, you need an element of marketing messaging throughout your sales conversation and the overall sales experience. Because these two functions are so heavily integrated, optimizing the success of your development strategy requires they be treated as a single function.

When we look at our business development initiatives at Tulip Media Group, it's all about landing new sales and optimizing growth. It doesn't matter if most of the weight was lifted by our marketing or by our sales initiatives, reducing the overall cost of acquisition is all that matters.

Therefore, the approach that we pivoted to was to one of not looking at it as a marketing initiative followed by a sales initiative but to instead view it all as a single growth initiative. It is all one business development strategy that we coined "SMarketing."

In this book, we are going to share with you the journey that we took and the changes that we made in our business development strategy that resulted in phenomenal success. Because we had success pursuing this new strategy and turning our business process on its head, we started sharing our success with our existing Client-Partners. We knew they were frustrated by where they were at, unable to break through into the next level of their growth trajectory. Not surprisingly, they wanted us to do the same thing for them with their companies. They knew they did not have a consistent and efficient process for bringing on new customers, and they saw the potential of growing their business the same way we did.

We offered to work with them to integrate a similar system into their companies. After experiencing comparable success with those first few early adopters and proving the integrity of the system, we have since expanded it and scaled it with many others.

Another factor that came into play for us was the events of 2020. The pandemic changed the way a lot of companies marketed because they could no longer rely on trade shows or conferences to go out and meet new potential customers. Instead, they had to find people online using different strategies than they were accustomed to. We became that alternative for these companies to pivot their business development strategy. They quickly discovered just how efficient and effective the SMarketing process can be.

With this new approach, we showed them how to bring down their cost of acquisition in 100 percent of cases by simply applying a SMarketing strategy to their business development processes. In this book, we'll explain in detail how we brought our cost of acquisition at Tulip Media Group down, from over $40,000 per new Client-Partner to under $4,000 in just 18 months. We'll show you how, in that same time frame, we cut our business development budget from over a million dollars a year to a fraction of that and how we've continued to grow sales at a faster rate ever since. Using these tools, we now help many of our Client-Partners accomplish similar results.

Here are a few examples of companies we've worked with:

- *Metalfab, a manufacturer of fire trucks, accelerated their sales through the pandemic while reducing costs. They did this by replacing trade shows as their primary strategy for lead generation to SMarketing, saving them tens of thousands of dollars and producing stronger results than they had experienced prior to the pandemic.*
- *Waypoint Insurance increased their customer inbound inquiries by 150 percent within four months of starting their SMarketing journey. At the same time, they cut their marketing costs in half! Their biggest challenge was having to hire more insurance agents to handle the increased opportunities that were coming to them using the new strategy.*
- *Homestead Road, a home buyer in FL, WI, and MN was successful in increasing their qualified pay-per-click leads by 79% in one quarter*

while saving an annualized amount of over $50,000 due to Google optimizations!

What about your company? Are you ready to gain some real momentum with an inbound marketing and sales strategy that will produce measurable results? Are you ready to engage your existing clients with a fully integrated digital and print marketing initiative that will create customer longevity and optimize referrals? Are you ready to stop chasing customers and let your market come to you by leveraging SMarketing for your business?

If you answered yes to any of the above, then this book is for you.

Chapter 1

Introduction By Andy Buyting

"All great changes are preceded by chaos." — Deepak Chopra

It was midafternoon on a warm Wednesday, May 8, 2019. I assembled our core Tulip Media team in the conference room and informed them I had just fired our entire sales department. At the time, the sales team accounted for nearly 35 percent of our staff.

Jaws dropped. The initial reaction was that of shock.

A few hours earlier, just after lunch, I had walked into our offices with a lump in my throat. After quietly assembling my notes in our conference room, I brought our entire sales team in, one by one, to speak with me. I then shared with them the extreme, excruciating and extraordinarily difficult decision we had made to let them all go.

I explained that the company was changing its strategy and taking a different approach to sales growth and business development. I made it clear that they were not at fault, but that it was a strategic decision that I and my two main business partners had made. And the decision was final.

This was an incredibly difficult thing to do. Over the years, we had grown to be a family, and I truly loved each person on our team. However, I knew with all my heart that this was the right decision for the company.

The Inspiration
The inspiration for this bold move came from a good friend of mine just

a couple of months earlier. At a business conclave in Boston, Patrick "Paddy" Condon shared the story of how he transformed his company, Finished Basements, in Denver, Colorado.

Finished Basements is a high-end home renovation company doing work in three cities: Denver, Minneapolis and Chicago. Paddy talked about how six months prior, he was doing annual planning with his team by way of a three-day event. During those three days, he and his partner drastically altered the structure of their business development strategy.

On the first day, they gathered the 12 people on their sales team together to strategize and discuss the future plans for the company. Doom and gloom filled the room. The sales team consistently blamed other departments and the company leaders for missing their sales targets, and Paddy had decided right there and then that he didn't want to continue that way.

One thing Paddy had always observed in their business was that when customers were speaking with the sales team, their defenses would go up. However, as soon as they were brought into the showroom to speak with a designer, they would begin to enjoy themselves. Instead of focusing on the deal, they would be focusing on the color schemes, the trim and the pot lights that would be used, and they would get very excited about starting the project with the designer. When customers were transferred back to the sales team, the magic disappeared instantly and their defenses would go right back up again.

In his words, the salespeople were often the ones killing sales deals!

On that day after meeting with the sales team, and growing increasingly frustrated, Paddy decided to execute on his new idea right there in the moment. He told his partner, "I'm willing to bet the entire company on this strategy: I want to let the entire sales team go, and I want the designers to sell jobs." Before the next morning, the two of them had called every single person on the sales team and let them go.

The next morning, they met with the designers and administration and told them what they had just done. Initially, everyone's instinct was to panic, but Paddy quickly explained his change in approach.

Paddy explained that nearly all of the inbound leads came from their marketing department, which was still fully staffed. He then explained that the designers would now be taking on the role of the salespeople in that they would be following up with customers, inviting them in to talk about their project and getting them excited to move forward.

When one of the designers declared that this sounded like a good plan but they weren't salespeople, Paddy replied, "Yes you are. In fact, you're better at selling than 'salespeople' are. You're the ones who get the people excited about their project through the design process. The only thing you need to do differently is this: when your customer is good with their design and budget, say: 'We're excited to get started! All we need is your signature here, and we'll get it scheduled.'"

Overnight, Paddy's best designers became his best salespeople. Customers were excited about their project, especially not having to deal with a "salesperson." Not only this but the company also cut about $2 million in costs! The new approach drastically changed the course of the business. In fact, sales went up by 12.5 percent that year.

This story really resonated with me. After being frustrated for five years with no end in sight, this story hit me between the eyes. At that moment, while hearing Paddy's story, I came to the same conclusion. We had to do something similar at Tulip Media.

I remember immediately walking out of that room in Boston and reaching out to my two main partners. I wanted to explore the idea of restructuring Tulip Media without a sales team.

As Tulip Media Group had grown, our outbound sales team had expanded to seven highly paid individuals including a sales manager. However, even though our team was growing and evolving its capabilities, it seemed that we were always falling short of quarterly sales targets and expectations. No matter what strategy, program, training or talent we brought into the organization, we could never seem to get ahead. In fact, through a return-on-investment lens, we were actually going backwards.

I knew there had to be a better way.

At the time, I had been toying with a new growth strategy that I described as building an "automated sales process." I knew the way we were growing our sales department was not working and that we needed to leverage online digital and automated sales strategies to create a truly profitable company. However, I also knew that to drastically change our business development strategy like this would mean that our entire company had to operate differently and that our salespeople would never go along for the ride.

That is why Paddy's story resonated so much for me.

I spoke with Paddy later that day to pick his brain. He challenged me to have the courage to destroy what's good in the pursuit of something great. It was a quote I had heard many times before.

That was all the encouragement I needed. That challenge from Paddy was the first step towards changing our business life forever.

The Great Pivot of 2019
On May 8, 2019, we flipped our business development model upside down. Up until that point, we'd had a good company that was growing at a consistent rate. We had grown the company using traditional marketing, attending conferences and trade shows, making thousands of cold calls, working referrals and more. We had a sales team seven-people strong, consisting of a sales manager and six salespeople. However, month after month, quarter after quarter, we would set sales targets and fall short. The more we grew, the lower our success rate for meeting these targets would get.

Our success rate fell so substantially that our cost of acquisition skyrocketed. It didn't happen overnight, but it did happen. In fact, the cost of acquisition at our worst point was over $40,000 for a new Client-Partner! In other words, our company was heading for bankruptcy if we didn't change something and change it drastically.

After that fateful day and hearing Paddy's story, I had a lot of deliberation and long conversations with my two main partners, which culminated in that business-altering Wednesday afternoon.

As soon as it was over and the entire sales team had been let go, I gathered the rest of the company and explained what I had done and why I had done it. I let them all in on the planning and the thought process that went into the decision.

We'd had an ineffective business growth model, and I took accountability for that. I then dove into the topic of what exactly I wanted to roll out and what my vision was for rolling it out. What I had always called an "automated sales process," Jessica Embree, my coauthor on this book, dubbed as SMarketing. After some discussion, everyone embraced this new vision.

A couple of days later, we went into our quarterly planning session. During the session, I let everyone know we were going to keep the same quarterly sales target going forward that we'd had for the past three quarters and consistently missed. I recall my right-hand person telling me I was crazy, pleading with me not to set us up for failure. However, I insisted that we keep the target going forward, that it would work. We had to make this work.

We moved forward and immediately started to implement our new SMarketing strategy. I replaced the sales team with a single junior marketing manager who believed anything was possible for our company. He was a recent university graduate that came to us during a co-op work program and stayed for the duration of the summer. It was just the high-energy start we needed. At the same time, Jessica, who handled a lot of marketing initiatives, was coming off her yearlong maternity leave and rejoining the company.

We were ready.

Tulip Media Group went from being an outbound sales organization—logging hundreds of phone calls and emails a week, following metrics on the number of calls, and expecting salespeople to make at least 30 outbound cold calls a day—to an organization that no longer made outbound cold calls at all. Can you believe that? Every single sales call we make now is because someone has reached out to us online and has scheduled their call in our calendars.

We went from chasing over 80 "qualified opportunities" a week to chasing twelve. We went from spending thousands and thousands of dollars every week on sales-related activities to dropping well under 10 percent of that.

To everyone's surprise, we hit our quarterly sales target for the first time in over a year. It was an incredible feeling. After that, we really knew we could do this.

We were succeeding by only speaking with people who raised their hand first. We were succeeding by only spending time, energy and resources on people who were truly interested in what we were doing.

This was a game changer for Tulip Media Group.

What we didn't realize was that it would also become a game changer for our Client-Partners in the months and years that followed. The incredible changes we've witnessed in our company and theirs since then are the reason Jessica and I wrote this book.

Chapter Two

A Broken System

"Insanity is doing the same thing over and over again and expecting different results." — Albert Einstein

Having worked in marketing for many years, we've seen firsthand the disconnect between marketing and sales. It's prolific. In almost every organization, the marketing and sales functions are separated, performed by different people or teams and motivated by different results. In addition to this separation, we see most business founders and entrepreneurs compound their growth challenges by devaluing the marketing function, pouring good money after bad (and a lot of it) only into sales.

In 90 percent of the cases we've seen, it's the sales department that has the bigger budget. It's the sales department that has the larger employment budget to hire more people, heftier compensation plans and lavish budgets to attend more conferences and trade shows. That's simply where the money is spent, albeit often unwisely, in many organizations.

The sales manager is often seen as one of the most important people in the organization. In those same organizations, there might be one young, part-time, recent college graduate stuck in a corner somewhere getting paid $30,000 a year to work under the banner of "marketing manager." On top of that, the marketing manager is not doing anything strategically important for the organization. Instead, they are focusing primarily on supporting sales with their latest requests like brochures or changes to wording on the website.

The sales team typically looks to marketing to back up their efforts. This is because they see sales as the one and only important function inside a company and believe it should be allocated the largest portion of the budget accordingly. Sales believes that everything should support their efforts because, naturally, they want to be as successful as they can be. This is admirable, but they demand so much support from marketing in their sales efforts that they prevent marketing from adding any real strategic value to the company's business development.

We've seen insurance agencies, healthcare facilities, law firms, manufacturers and professional service providers spend endless amounts of money on call centers, travel allowances for mobile salespeople, and everything else under the sun to support sales. Sales always seems to have this massive budget, but when it comes to marketing, the budget falls to five, 10, maybe 20 percent of what the sales budget is. That says a lot about the way these two departments are traditionally handled. To us, a company that looks like that is missing a huge opportunity.

What we know, and what has been proven repeatedly if you've paid any attention to recent business successes, is this: marketing should and needs to have a place at the table. In fact, marketing, in most cases, is actually strategically more important than most other departments in an organization.

Milan Kundera is famous, in part, for saying, "Business has only two functions: marketing and innovation." A strong business starts by producing new products and services that add value to customers' lives and then leveraging marketing to spread the word and to grow sales.

Joe Polish, one of the biggest marketing gurus around, said that any problem can be solved with the right sales letter. In other words, any problem in the world can be solved with the right messaging. How powerful is that? That's marketing!

Marketing shouldn't be the last thing you want to do as an organization, something that you feel obligated to do in order to support your sales team. In our experience, when marketing reaches this point, the cost of acquisitions skyrockets and the organization loses traction.

It's unfortunate that the business world has created this divisiveness between sales and marketing, and the process continues to be broken down further and further. There are even companies you can hire to perform lead generation and cold-calling services as part of your marketing budget. Ironically, the answer for rapid, scalable success actually lies in moving in the other direction. That's why when you continue to spend those extra dollars on these types of initiatives, you're probably not seeing the results that you expect. Marketing and sales do not operate in silos. In fact, they work much better together as part of a single business development strategy.

We know all this first hand because we've done it. We've been there, making that same mistake. Years ago, we hired one of those cold-calling companies ourselves. We invested a lot of our marketing dollars to hire an outside firm to perform lead generation for us. The firm required a massive retainer of several thousand dollars each month plus six hundred dollars every time they sent a "qualified lead" our way.

Of course, our sales team loved it. They were getting qualified leads handed to them without having to do any of the legwork or worrying about the cost of acquiring those leads. The problem? We weren't closing any of those outside leads.

Was it because of our salespeople? Maybe. But mostly, it was because they weren't really qualified leads to begin with. The lead generation firm was not incentivized by how many deals we closed, only the number of leads they provided to us that we accepted. Their firm was paid on quantity, not quality.

From this experience, we learned that marketing should not be treated as a separate function. When you treat marketing as a separate function, you will continue to waste money on services that produce little to no real results.

If your current sales and marketing budget isn't returning you new business, your company is missing out and will never live up to its full potential. If one of your competitors gets wind of that, you'll be dead in the water, losing your market share at an alarming rate.

Unfortunately, in most organizations, that's just the way it is. The salespeople have the highest budget while they are incentivized primarily to keep their own engine running. They are given little reason to worry about the needs of the organization as a whole, and the organization suffers as a result.

Part of the problem is that salespeople don't want marketing to get too powerful or strategic because it encroaches on their own sales budgets and may even outshine them. As a result, marketing stays in the background with a supporting role, careful not to chew too far into the sales budget. When companies have this mind-set and model, it creates conflict within the company and stunts growth.

If your company is employing this technique, in most industries, we guarantee you are suffering because of it. Marketing needs to be strategic in every business, yet far too many companies don't see it that way. Compartmentalizing your sales and marketing means you are wasting tens of thousands if not millions of dollars a year driving a barrier between the two. Instead, you should be working to drive them in sync with a tailored SMarketing process.

In the early days of Tulip Media Group, one of our partners challenged Andy by saying, "If you were a 20-something person fresh out of university just starting out, would you hire all these salespeople? If you were just starting out, would you build this massive sales team with these massive sales budgets? These are some of the highest paid people in the company. Would you choose to do that again and go to market that way?" Of course, the answer was no.

Sam Walton, the founder of Walmart, recognized back in the late 1980s that Walmart was growing and quickly becoming one of the largest companies in the world. At the time, Walton was displacing companies like Sears and Kmart (remember them?). He knew this was due in large part to his strategy and his own shrewdness in his approach to business. These once "superior" companies were struggling to compete with Walmart because they were using traditional business processes and strategy, including traditional sales and marketing models. Meanwhile, Walmart was trying something new.

Walton recognized that no company lasts forever because the world of business is constantly evolving. Even Walmart, he anticipated, would eventually be displaced by some young start-up that would reinvent the business model again. Walmart would be displaced by "two guys in a garage," so to speak, and Walton acknowledged that.

What if you looked at your company with a fresh set of eyes, with none of the history, legacy, people and personalities around the table that you have now? Knowing what you know now, if you were starting out fresh, young and fearless in your company today, bold and ready to destroy what's good in the pursuit of what's great, would you build up a sales team like you have today? Would the same things comprise your sales engine if you had the chance to do it all over again? Our guess is that you would probably do it differently.

We want to be clear that we're not advocating for firing your entire sales team in one day like we did. We're not advocating that at all because it might not be the right approach for your company, your industry and your unique business model. It was right for us, but it's not going to be right for everyone, and that's okay.

What we are asking you to do is to question your model, to question your go-to market strategy and your business development strategy. Is it working? How much money are you wasting? How often do you exceed your quarterly sales goals? Could you do it differently and make it better?

If you knew as much as you know now about your industry and the products and services that you deliver but had a fresh view on the world and the possibilities for SMarketing, would you go about your business development strategy differently? We think you would.

Think about it another way. If somebody were to come along in your marketplace that approaches sales and marketing in a new way, leveraging new digital marketing techniques, would you be nervous right now? If the product and service they were delivering was of equal quality and value to yours but they had an alternative go-to-market strategy that was creating waves in your industry, would you be worried?

If the answer is yes, then it's time to reconsider your sales and marketing strategy. It's time to consider bringing marketing to the forefront. If you truly embrace marketing for what it should be, that in itself is one of the most powerful strategies that you can have and develop within your company.

Business is all about communication. At the end of the day, business is all about sending the right message to the right people. You're communicating with customers so they'll buy your product or service. You're communicating with employees so they'll be motivated to work and to grow with your company. You're communicating with all of your stakeholders so they have faith in your company and your ability to grow. Whether you're in a business-to-business or business-to-consumer model, at the end of the day, you are communicating human-to-human. It's all about communication, and it's all about meaningful interaction with each other. That's what business is.

Communication and marketing are one in the same; marketing is communication and communication is marketing. In this book, we're going to talk about customer-facing communication, but you can translate these concepts into employee and stakeholder communication because that's marketing too.

When we're talking about marketing and messaging and what your brand stands for, we would argue that it's among the most important strategic decisions that you can make in your company. How you choose to go to market will set the tone for your cost structure, your business model, your customer engagement and your overall company strategy.

You can see that, given the significance of marketing as a core competency in securing new business, it deserves to be treated as a strategic part of the business. Marketing deserves to have a seat at the strategic table and a budget that reflects its value, especially when it comes to your business development strategy.

In the 1980s, it was the Chief Financial Officer who took the right-hand seat to the CEO as the controller of the corporate purse strings. As we moved into the 2000s and the war on talent became a reality, Human Resources became one of the most strategic and key positions in the organization. Now that we're into the 2020s, the power has shifted to marketing and an organization's ability to communicate effectively to achieve its purpose. Communication is one of the most critical strategies for staying competitive in the ever-evolving market as we know it.

When you get marketing right, the rest often falls into place. By combining your sales and marketing, your business development, human resources, production and delivery can all run much more smoothly. It's that simple.

So, look at your business again and ask yourself: If you were to create your company all over again knowing what you know now, would you do it differently? If your answer is yes, let's talk about SMarketing.

Chapter Three

Your Business Development Assembly Line

"Sales is the responsibility of a centrally-coordinated team."
— Justin Roff-Marsh

Combining your sales and marketing into a SMarketing model begins with building your business development assembly line. This will require you to completely change the way you look at your business development processes.

If you're like most companies, you started out with a product or service that you wanted to sell. A network was slowly formed to meet with potential customers and clientele. You hired a firm to produce a small number of brochures and marketing materials.

As the business grew, demands on your time became too much. More help was needed to sell so your company hired its first salesperson. The new salesperson went out into the market to sell your products and services. They did so with slightly less passion but were keen to sell all the same. In time, a second and third salesperson were hired.

You taught each new salesperson everything they needed to know about the company, from the products or services you sell to your customers and the marketplace. Throughout this, you likely explained the sales process as a "sales playbook" and showed them how to perform each of the steps required, from finding prospects all the way to closing sales.

Each salesperson probably approached sales in much the same way: they went out, found leads and potential customers, met new potential clients, understood prospects' needs and how your company could serve them and talked to these prospects about your company and the products and services you offer. Maybe this required five to six phone calls and a couple of meetings over the lifespan of your sales cycle.

For those prospects that showed some kind of interest in what your company had to sell or that indicated they might have a problem your company could help solve, your salesperson would schedule a time to sit down with them in person or to discuss it over the phone. They would take this opportunity to get to know your prospect and really zero in on the problem they were looking to solve.

If this initial meeting went well, your salesperson would schedule a product demonstration to showcase your product or service. They would then book a strategy meeting to discuss how your solution could integrate into their life or into their business, depending on whether your company is a B2C or B2B model.

Does all of this sound familiar so far?

After the strategy call, your salesperson probably went back for a confirmation call or two to answer any questions the prospect had. This could mean talking to someone else at the prospect's firm—the decision maker or other users of your product or solution—to get the final go ahead.

Finally, your salesperson would reach a point where they knew that what they were selling met the customer's needs and would move in to close the sale. Once the deal had been closed, they would transfer the customer to your accounting department to process the sale, bill them and charge the commission for that salesperson.

That would be a typical eight-step sales process.

Now, for just a moment, let's shed the notion that this is what a standard sales process should look like. Let's look at your sales process instead through a different lens.

Think back to the early 1900s when Henry Ford, grandfather of assembly lines and high-volume manufacturing, made the automobile affordable for anyone who wanted to own their own car. He achieved this phenomenon through the use of assembly lines. Henry Ford did not invent the automobile; he invented the process that drove down the cost of manufacturing and made the automobile accessible to the masses.

The logic here is simple. If you were just launching an automobile manufacturing company today, you would not have a single craftsperson source the raw materials, create all the different parts, assemble the entire vehicle, finish the exterior, package the vehicle for delivery and ship the finished vehicle out to the customer. That just wouldn't make sense.

Instead, you would break the process down into segments and assign the various tasks to different people. You would have someone in charge of sourcing the raw material, someone else in charge of managing logistics, several specialists stationed at various points along the manufacturing assembly line, each doing their part. This allows people to specialize and become very good at their segment of the manufacturing process. The objective here is to use everyone's talents at maximum capacity and to achieve the highest return on investment on their time.

Despite not being in the manufacturing industry, Andy started applying this same approach to Tulip Media Group in 2019 after his business coach introduced him to a book called *The Machine* by Justin Roff-Marsh. Instead of looking at business development as a linear function being performed by the same person beginning to end, *The Machine* looks at the business development process as a machine, so to speak, and advocates an assembly-line approach to selling.

The first step to creating a business development assembly line in your company is to break down the various steps within your selling process. It requires you to really put your processes under scrutiny and think about how to group tasks into specialized jobs.

When doing this, we want you to consider every single step required to close sales. This includes steps prior to your salespeople talking to prospects, such as researching and prospecting, as well as steps after they've confirmed a close and signed the paperwork, collected payment, etc. Your business development assembly line needs to encompass everything involved in growing your sales.

At Tulip Media Group, we broke our sales process down into eight steps, or specific jobs, each requiring different competencies and specialized skills. This is what worked for our company, but note that you may identify more or fewer steps in your own process and that's okay. Every business is different.

Tulip Media Group's Eight-Step Sales Process
1. *Prospecting New Leads*
2. *Lead Generation*
3. *Introductory Meeting*
4. *Product Demo*
5. *Strategy Session*
6. *Confirmation Call*
7. *Finishing Call*
8. *Close the Sale*

Most companies have a sales process already, whether it is formal or informal. The difference is that most companies, including Tulip Media Group prior to May 2019, have the same salespeople handle all eight steps of the process. Using this traditional approach, a team of "generalists" performs in several different roles that require very different skills and competencies. This results in the process being much less efficient and the whole system being less successful, closing fewer sales than it should.

In a functional business development assembly line approach, each step needs to be optimized with the right people. The analogy Andy uses is that when you're playing a team sport, you all focus on doing what you're good at to get the goal. No one expects a single player to play every position. Every player is assigned to play the position they're good at and where they can contribute the most. Ultimately, the whole team succeeds by doing things this way.

As an example, Andy is an excellent closer, but he struggles with prospecting. That's why we let Andy close many of the deals but have others who are better at building an early rapport do the prospecting and initiate the early discussions. It only makes sense. This way Andy can spend just a few hours a week working on sales activities and close millions of dollars in new business each year, making the entire team so much more successful than it otherwise would.

When we looked at the way we were doing things prior to May 2019, it was clear that we were not optimizing anything about how we sold. For us, implementing a business development assembly line approach meant letting our entire sales team go and reorganizing our team to play in the positions where they were strongest.

When composing our new strategy, Andy couldn't concern himself with the interests of the sales team because the interests of the sales team no longer aligned with the interests of the organization as a whole. To succeed in the transition to this new model, we needed to look at our business development process as a unified team initiative instead of continuing to cultivate individual players who acted independently from each other and from the organization.

When you break down your own business development assembly line, keep your sales team out of mind. We aren't suggesting that you let your entire sales team go like we did, but you don't want to create jobs just for the sake of accommodating the people and personalities on your team. Once you're clear on the positions you need filled (the stations in your business development assembly line), you want to assign people to jobs that play to their strengths and make the company stronger and more successful at closing deals. Break down your process first, then think about your people.

The people you choose to specialize in each step of your business development assembly line should be especially talented in their assigned area. Let's say that one of your salespeople is really good at opening doors with prospects. This person is especially talented at making contact with potential customers and generating that initial interest in purchasing. However, they aren't especially talented at researching, controlling the sales process or even closing the deal. In this case, that talented prospector should be prospecting all the time. That's what's going to provide you with the greatest return on investment and contribute the most to the unified team efforts to sell. Doesn't it make more sense to have them focus solely on what they're good at?

Hire someone else who is really good at researching to do the research. Another talented person could be responsible for product demonstrations and answering questions about the intricacies of how the product or service works. The product demonstration specialist could then send the client over to a specialized strategist who can help them really understand what a program including your product or service would look like for them. Once the strategist is finished talking to them, they could send the client to talk to someone who is really talented at closing. Wouldn't that be more effective? After the closer has a verbal agreement, you can quickly hand that order off to accounting to sign the contract and receive payment while your closer goes out and closes another client who's been passed down your business development assembly line.

If you are worried that this sounds like there are "too many cooks in the kitchen" during the sales process and your potential customers are being passed from one specialist to another, we want to remind you to do what makes sense for your business. In our eight-step example above, however, our prospects are typically only meeting two to three people on our team. We've automated most of the early steps, and the other specialists are involved behind the scenes.

Business development truly is a team sport. On a hockey team, a good offensive player is not a good defenseman. A good center does not make a good goalie. A defenseman should not be counted on to score goals. These dynamics prevail in business as well. When everyone on the team plays their designated part well, the team wins.

Your company would simply be better served if there were different people who specialize in every step of the sales journey. It's a complete waste of time and resources to have the same person doing everything from beginning to end. Instead, build the steps in your business development assembly line, find what your people are good at, understand where they excel and have them specialize in their one or two stations along that assembly line. This is a natural solution to increasing efficiency and the success rate of your business development process.

Think of it this way: Where would your business be if your best closer could be out there closing 80 percent of the time, ensuring you never miss a deal? We're guessing a lot further ahead than you are now.

The Machine also talks about real time spent selling. If you tracked how much time your salespeople actually spent selling, you would probably be unpleasantly surprised. Selling, by definition, is interacting with a prospect. In order to be actively engaged in the selling process, your salespeople need to be actively engaged with a prospect, whether that's interacting virtually, on the phone or in a meeting. Whatever the medium, your salespeople should be consistently moving the sales process forward through customer engagement. That's their job.

Researching new prospects is not selling. Chasing people via phone or email to set up that next meeting is not selling. If you discount these activities from real time spent selling, how much of the time are your salespeople truly selling to prospects? On average, the answer to this question is a meager 6%–15%. Yikes. This means that your highly paid salespeople are only producing at their highest level 6%–15% of the time. What a poor return on your investment.

Instead, why not have your closers, prospectors and demonstration people focus on what they are each really good at? This way, they can add the greatest possible value to the organization all the time while you have others at a lower pay grade play supporting roles. Doesn't that just make sense?

We challenge you now to think through your business development process and identify your own steps. What is the sales process for your company and how can it be broken down to create a business development assembly line? Start to think about who the right people might be to specialize in each job.

Looking at your business development process as an assembly line is the first step to combining your sales and marketing processes and executing a SMarketing strategy. The objective here should be to identify the people or processes most suitable to perform each function along the way and to decide who or what will have the most success, the maximum impact and the greatest return on investment at each station.

Before you move on to the next chapter, write down the steps you've identified in your business development process. Figure out how many steps there are and what kind of person might be a high-performing contributor for each of those steps. We'll delve further into how to build and optimize your business development assembly line—or machine—in the next chapter.

Chapter Four

Building & Optimizing Your Machine

"In the Infinite Game we accept that "being the best" is a fool's errand and that multiple players can do well at the same time." – Simon Sinek

Now that we've established that your selling process should really be treated as a business development assembly line, every step along that assembly line needs to be built and optimized. To do this, we first need to assess the appropriate people and processes for each station.

When we embarked on our own journey to combine sales and marketing at Tulip Media, we made the decision to automate a large portion of our selling process. Looking back at Henry Ford's original assembly line, we saw that, over time, the roles of many people were replaced with machines and robotics. This wasn't necessarily to reduce the head count; instead, it ensured that each station was running at the highest degree of predictability and efficiency.

When processes can be automated, it often becomes inefficient and ineffective to utilize human resources in these roles. A craftsperson should not be wasting time screwing nuts and bolts onto the automobile when they could be designing a state-of-the-art interior, which is something that a machine cannot do. In the same way, you don't want your talented employees wasting their time performing processes that could be automated. While they could certainly perform reasonably well at such activities, the payoff just isn't there when you could utilize technology at a fraction of the cost. Having broken your assembly line down into stations, the objective is now going to be to optimize each step and automate as much as possible.

In our case, we managed to automate almost the entire first half of our selling process using our SMarketing model. Researching qualified leads, lead generation and scheduling introductory calls have all been automated thanks to the many digital tools available to us. For many prospects, we have even automated our product demonstrations with videos. This frees up our knowledgeable production managers and digital marketing strategists to optimize and really make an impact in our strategy meetings and confirmation calls with prospects. It can also be very convenient for prospects because they can watch a 10- to 20-minute demonstration video on their own time instead of setting aside 40 minutes or more for a live Zoom call demo. Following the strategy meeting and confirmation call, other team members step in to close the deal and process contracts.

Below, we've outlined our business development assembly line and what person or process we've put in place for each station in our line.

Tulip Media Group's Eight-Step Sales Process and
Our Tactic for Each Step

1.	*Prospecting New Leads*	*Inbound Digital Marketing*
2.	*Lead Generation*	*StoryBrand Landing Pages*
3.	*Introductory*	*Meeting Short Form Content (Written & Videos)/Phone Consults*
4.	*Product Demo*	*Live Zoom Demo or Video Recording*
5.	*Strategy Session*	*Live Zoom Call or Strategy Session*
6.	*Confirmation Call*	*Live Zoom/Phone Call to Answer Questions*
7.	*Finishing Call*	*Live Zoom/Phone Call to Close the Deal*
8.	*Close the Sale*	*Signing Paperwork & Receiving Payment*

Step one in our business development assembly line was always to research qualified leads. In order to do this, we used to buy industry lists, attend trade shows and conferences, scour the internet constantly for prospects and make endless phone calls trying to find new potential leads. We don't do any of that anymore. Now, we find qualified leads entirely through the digital marketing techniques our company specializes in. This means all of the work is automated and done for us.

Step two of our assembly line was lead generation. For us, this meant persuading a potential prospect to agree to a phone call. We used to spend hundreds of hours sending out emails and making cold calls. We would fork out thousands of dollars each week to buy expensive promotional packages that we would FedEx to all of the qualified leads on our list. Occasionally, we would receive a response from someone interested in learning more about what we had to offer, but, realistically, this approach wasn't sustainable. We've now replaced this component of the process with our digital marketing and online conversion strategies.

Online conversions work hand in hand with the digital marketing that brings leads to our website and various landing pages. At Tulip Media Group, we are one of 40 Certified StoryBrand Agencies. Each web page is specifically designed using StoryBrand methodology to convert the audience we're targeting. We use messaging that meets the prospect where they are so that we can connect to and engage with them through a specific call to action.

Typically, after an expression of interest, our next step is to schedule an introductory call. This is an opportunity for us to learn more about the prospect as much as it is an opportunity for them to learn more about us. A typical 30-minute introductory call starts with 25 minutes talking about the prospect, their company, their market, their business goals. This helps us identify the gap between their current trajectory and where they want to go. In those last five minutes of the call, if we feel that our solutions are a potential fit for their business, we simply let them know that we believe we can help them out and that we should plan a demonstration.

We also have an automated introductory call option for prospects, which saves us hundreds of hours on calls that don't convert and often provides added flexibility that is welcomed by the prospect. We do this by providing short-form content that offers some key pieces of information about our services, our company and in what situations our solutions can make the biggest impact. The messaging is formatted with a combination of text, video and infographics that gives prospects the option to consume this information in the format that is best suited to them. Many prospects will self-select out of our sales funnel after consuming this information.

However, if they continue, we know we have a good chance of closing.

Step four in our process is program demonstrations. In our SMarketing strategy, we automate these demonstrations as much as we can by giving prospects the option to learn even more about our offerings through samples, longer-form content and videos. However, most of our demonstrations still happen by video call because this enables us to share with prospects directly how we can help their company grow and strategize about their business specifically.

If a prospect opts for the live demonstration, they will speak directly with someone in production, typically a production manager. If the production manager feels the prospect could benefit from specific expertise, such as search engine optimization, pay-per-click advertising or website conversion strategy, they can bring someone else from our production team into the demonstration with them, even if the second team member only drops in for part of the demo. We've found that the best people to provide thorough answers to a prospect's questions are those who are working in that area of service delivery every day. This works so much better than having a general salesperson who requires assistance to provide detailed answers to most questions.

We also find that a prospect's guard goes down when they talk to someone in production instead of to a salesperson. A conversation with a salesperson too often feels like the prospect is simply being sold to. With a production manager or marketing specialist, potential Client-Partners enjoy talking about their marketing strategy and envisioning what we can do for their company. Our SMarketing approach creates a more enjoyable and relaxing sales experience for everyone involved.

From there, we get into a strategy discussion. This part is not automated because we trust that if a prospect has gone through a demonstration, then they are ready to book a serious call with a specialist on our team to discuss their specific needs. The person they talk to will be a specialist in understanding their needs, strategizing with them on their marketing and relating how we can help them achieve their business growth goals. In our company, these calls often involve one of our marketing specialists. They are the best fit to quickly disseminate the prospect's current trajectory, what their objectives are, the gap between the two and how our programs can best help them close that gap and meet those objectives.

By the time we book this strategy call, we've already done a lot of research on the prospect both directly and through our automated processes. The information we collected early on with our automated processes creates an advantage for us here and tells us our prospect has jumped through a few of our hoops and self-qualified. If they hadn't been interested enough in our programs to navigate their way to this point, it wouldn't be worth our time to pursue them. The strategy call is a milestone for both our company and theirs.

The automated portion of our selling process is designed to filter out those who are not qualified and who would not make quality Client-Partners. Sometimes a prospect does not have an appropriate budget or a timeline conducive for our programs to help. Other times, the need really isn't there and our solutions are not a good fit for their business. We remedy these potential issues by understanding and having answers to BANT right away. If you are not familiar, BANT stands for **B**udget, **A**uthority, **N**eed, and **T**imeline and we highly recommend incorporating it into your selling process.

Budget
Right from the beginning, we share with the prospect rough budgets required for our programs. This way, they can opt out of our sales process early on if their budget isn't a fit. If the figures are more than they're willing to invest, this person can walk away before the strategy call without any pressure to buy, and we won't have used up any time pursuing a sale that will never close.

Authority
To serve the authority piece, we ask for the decision maker to be on the strategy call with us. We do this any time we initiate a call involving strategy or changes to Client-Partner programs. Having this safeguard in place protects us from dealing with someone who is interested in using our programs for their company but has yet to persuade those with decision-making power.

Need

If there isn't a true need for our programs and services in their company, it makes no sense for us to waste anyone's time. The most common reason a prospect will self-select out of our sales funnel is that they were searching for business development strategies, and after finding our website, they realized that our programs really didn't fit their company's needs. With our process set up this way, we presume that if they've made it to a strategy call, they do have a need for our programs, and we will explore and confirm this again during that call.

Timeline

Finally, we discuss the timeline and ensure that we can meet their expectations. When a prospect books an online demonstration or strategy call, we ask right away when they would like their program to launch, if we do in fact move forward together. Although we've handled some very tight timelines at Tulip Media, we always like to be prepared.

When we show up to the strategy meeting prepared to have a conversation around BANT with a strategist who knows exactly what they're doing, it makes for a very productive discussion.

The strategy call is the most important and impactful call in our selling process. Leading up to the call, we have already learned a lot about the prospect, and we've identified the gap between their current trajectory and their growth objectives. They are also going into the call with a fairly deep understanding of our program offerings. This allows everyone to then work collaboratively on developing a specific strategy that is going to suit their needs.

When we work collaboratively to build out their strategy, we are bringing our years of deep marketing expertise to the table; however, they are also bringing their years of deep industry expertise to the discussion. This allows us to build out a strategy that is not only unique to them but is also built by both parties. By doing so, and allowing them to essentially "co-build" their solution with us, they have a sense of ownership and investment into our relationship before we ever ask for the sale. This is what makes the strategy session so impactful. In many ways, our strategy session, step five in our sales process, is the most important conversation we're going to have with a prospect. When done correctly, and both sides see a good fit and feel good about the strategy we've created together, we are all but guaranteed to close that sale.

Following the strategy session, we let the prospect digest our discussion and sleep on their new marketing strategy. That's why we'll often book our confirmation call, step six in our sales process, one to three days after our strategy call.

For us, often the same person that handles strategy calls will handle confirmation calls. These two components are very much related in nature. While the strategy call is meant to co-build a marketing strategy together and will illustrate what a Client-Partner relationship with us might look like, the confirmation call is an opportunity for the prospect to ask any questions they may have and receive a thorough, tailored response to each one. Usually these questions arise after they've had a chance to reflect on the strategy we created together in the previous session.

The seventh step in our selling process is our finishing call. This is typically done by the production manager and often involves Andy as well. If Andy is needed to close a deal, the strategist briefs Andy on the company and the strategies they've created together. Andy can then share his enthusiasm, answer any final questions they may have and ask for the sale.

One of the reasons this works so well is because of the message it conveys to the prospect. When a production manager or specialist informs the prospect we are excited about the opportunity to work with their company and to help them grow, it conveys interest. However, when that same production manager or specialist informs the prospect they are so excited that they've spoken with the CEO about them and that the CEO would really love to meet them, that makes the prospect feel really special. It's at that time Andy jumps on the call, talks knowledgeably about their business, conveys his confidence in the program we've come up with and asks for the sale.

Once we get a verbal commitment, a contract is issued immediately using a proprietary pricing and automated contract generation tool we've created and the deal moves straight over to accounting. They are responsible for getting everything signed and issuing the first invoice for payment.

We make this final step as simple as possible for our Client-Partners. Our contracts are short, easy to understand and issued using an online signature platform to facilitate quick and easy execution.

Just like that, it's a wrap.

By building our sales funnel in this way, we have effectively automated the first three to four steps of our business development assembly line, saving us hundreds of thousands of dollars each year. Having three to four different people involved in the remaining four or five steps means each person is being employed in their highest payoff activities and nothing more. Each person is working within their native genius, providing the highest return on investment for their time and not wasting resources on activities that should be done by others or automated.

By taking this approach and implementing a SMarketing strategy for Tulip Media Group, we successfully reduced our cost of acquisition by over 90 percent in just 18 months.

Case Study

An example of a similar streamlined selling process can be found in our Client-Partner company, Metalfab Fire Trucks. Metalfab is a manufacturer of custom fire trucks, and their selling process requires a specialized approach because their audience is so unique. We knew a SMarketing strategy would be an excellent fit.

Because Metalfab decided to aim outside of larger cities and mainstream communities for their target audience, we needed to cast a wide net to attract fire chiefs from smaller communities in the market for a new fire truck. What makes this target audience unique is that they only enter the market for a new truck once or twice every 10 to

20 years, so selling can become very tricky. A traditional outbound marketing strategy would certainly have been inefficient.

As we researched further, we discovered that fire chiefs are more easily captured for a sale while they're looking for information before they start their buying journey. To accommodate this, we helped Metalfab use online content marketing to position them as an industry expert and draw prospects in. Metalfab recognized that fire chiefs, who would only be in the market for a new fire truck once every 10 years or so, needed to essentially re-educate themselves every time they bought a new truck. With our help, Metalfab became a resource for information on the many new fire truck-related technologies that potential buyers would be interested to know about.

Metalfab also discovered that the company's success rate skyrocketed when they were communicating with fire chiefs before they went to tender. For this reason, we helped them to create messaging and a call-to-action for fire chiefs looking for resources on how to write a request for proposal (RFP) document. We then launched a pay-per-click marketing campaign on Google targeting fire chiefs looking for information on writing a good RFP, pointing them to the company's landing page. This automated the conversion process and funneled an abundance of potential customers Metalfab's way.

When you're developing your own sales and marketing strategy, you need to keep an open mind. Ask yourself how you would start up and create a new business development process if you were launching your company all over again. For the time being, forget about personalities, forget about your salespeople and those working with you, and forget about what you've done in the past. We want you to think about your future.

Don't dissuade yourself with statements like: "Well, this is how I've always done it." That is a bad answer. Equally bad is telling yourself: "We've invested so much in our current sales process and team, and I'm not about to throw that away." That's a sunk cost, and you shouldn't allow that to impede on current decisions.

As Simon Sinek would say, you need to have an infinite mind-set and look at it for the long haul. Take that infinite mind-set and continually tweak and refine your processes to stay competitive in the ever-evolving business playing field. Remember that business is a game with no end. It goes on perpetually and infinitely, and you need to be swift and responsive to stay on top.

In our case, being swift and responsive meant taking the leap with a streamlined SMarketing strategy. It has boosted our margins like you wouldn't believe, and that's why we've recommended it to all of our Client-Partners.

A strong SMarketing strategy starts with a well-defined, populated and optimized business development assembly line. The first step for building your own business development assembly line is to explore what the right steps for your selling process are. Then you can take your new assembly line, ask yourself what can be automated with technology and online resources, and decide how your remaining steps could be optimized with the right people doing the right jobs within your new strategy.

When you're assessing your team's talent for the right fit in your business development assembly line, it's sometimes better to work backwards from the last step to the first. Take stock of the talent you have available on your team and map out how different specialists could best work and optimize each station. This will be tricky, and it might take a few tries to get it right.

As you get to the first half of your selling process, consider how you might automate each step instead of assigning talent. When you're finished, up to half of your selling process should hopefully be automated, with the remainder employing your team at their highest payoff activities. If you've done this effectively, you will see your success rates increase exponentially with the same or fewer people than you have now. As time goes on and you experience new growth, you can expand your team by hiring based on the specific competencies you need at each station on your assembly line.

Chapter Five

Discovering Your Core Customer

---

*"Your Core Customer is a **real** individual with a unique identity and needs."*
– Dr. Robert Bloom

When you establish your business development assembly line and select the talent or automation you want to employ at each station, you are ultimately working to optimize your customer journey. The customer journey is, of course, influenced by the entire selling process. If you have unqualified people or inefficient systems working at any part of your assembly line, it will quickly translate into a poor experience for your customers and fewer sales.

When you consider your customer journey, you need to think about what the buying experience looks and feels like for your customers. Put yourself in your customer's shoes and view the process through their lens. Decide for yourself the quality of your customer journey. Is it frictionless or is it problematic?

If you have customers that are falling through the cracks, that don't understand the benefits of engaging with your products and services, or that find it difficult to interact with your systems, your customer journey needs work. As Donald Miller, author of *Building a StoryBrand*, would say, "If you confuse, you lose." Each customer should progress seamlessly through your selling process, understand the benefits of working with you fully and feel excited to interact with you at each stage of the process. The goal is to make the journey as frictionless as possible.

There are several steps to creating a frictionless customer journey, but first, you need to get to know and really understand your core customer. This is what we'll focus on here. If you are unfamiliar with the concept, your core customer is the person most likely to purchase your product or service. Not only this, but your core customer is the one who values your product or service the most and is willing to buy from you at the highest price, optimizing your profitability. By understanding your core customer, you empower your company to maximize revenues by attracting the people that will provide the greatest return for your company.

One thing to note for those in the B2B space is that when we address the core customer, we are addressing the person directly, not the business. Yes, you do need to understand the demographics of the businesses your company targets; however, it is not the business who's going to make the decision to buy from you, it's a person inside that business. This is why you need to understand the real person and connect directly with them.

Most companies attempt to understand their core customer by simply defining the demographic of the person they want to attract. Marketing managers typically consider those demographics and may even create a customer avatar, but then they stop there. This is a great start, but it is only the first step in truly understanding your core customer. At Tulip Media Group, we follow a comprehensive process developed by Donald Miller, founder and developer of StoryBrand, for understanding and communicating with our clients' core customer.

The StoryBrand methodology takes you several steps beyond defining the demographics of your core customer. Building your customer avatar is just one of several components that go into what Donald Miller calls your StoryBrand BrandScript. The BrandScript framework guides you through an entire process to fully understand the psyche of your core customer so that you can meet them where they're at and connect with them quickly. It focuses on the message you are sending to your core customer and creates connectivity and consistency in your selling process. This enables you to connect with your core customer on a deeper level and encourages them to buy from you at every stage of their journey. The process works so well that in 2020, Tulip Media Group opted to certify our entire team based on this methodology and become a StoryBrand Certified Agency.

Your BrandScript starts with defining the character of your core customer. Who is it you're trying to reach and what do they want? What problem do they have that you can solve? What are they looking for in you? You need to have a full understanding of these things before you can formulate a message that will attract your core customer and design a customer journey that will provide them with the greatest buying experience.

When you're trying to communicate with your core customer through a digital marketing strategy or through any kind of advertising, you have very little time to make a connection and sink the hook to keep their attention. When you think of the best TV shows and blockbuster movies you've seen, you'll notice that within the first 90 seconds, they hook the viewer with some form of conflict. If they didn't do this, they would start to lose your attention. It happens very quickly, and in marketing, the change happens even faster. This means you need to introduce conflict in your prospect's mind as early on as possible in your marketing messaging.

To do this effectively, you need to first understand who or what your core customer's problem is. Once you find the root cause of your customer's problem, you can personify what it is that they're dealing with. This provides the conflict element for your messaging. Quite often, it's actually not what you think, so spend some time performing a thorough analysis here.

At Tulip Media Group, we used to think the problem our potential Client-Partners had was their competition, that what they were most stressed out about when it came to their marketing was battling their competitors. Once we went further in our analysis, however, we realized their external problem was really the confusing world of marketing, so we strategically changed our approach to communicating with them.

When you think about it, online marketing is so complicated and so complex that most small business owners and marketing managers find it difficult to understand. The idea of marketing online creates confusion, frustration and a feeling of being overwhelmed. When we analyzed the problem our Client-Partners were dealing with, we determined that one of the factors contributing to their problem was a lack of knowledge about how to market in the digital world.

Our Client-Partners didn't even know where to get started when it came to marketing online. As a result, they were feeling confused and overwhelmed with their marketing. This was our opportunity to really connect with them. We strategically aligned our messaging with this problem so that we could meet our customers where they were at, connect with what they were thinking at the moment and create that connection very quickly. This became the early messaging in our BrandScript.

After you've broken the problem down for your core customer, Miller recommends introducing yourself as the guide without positioning yourself as the hero. Too many companies make the mistake of coming in like a knight in shining armor declaring, "You've got a problem, we can help. We're coming in on our white horse and we're going to save the day." That is the wrong approach. You are not the hero of the story, your customer is. You are merely the guide, the person who can help them get where they want to go. They are Luke Skywalker and you are Yoda.

When you position yourself as the guide, you then allow them to be the hero of their own movie. When you come in as the knight in shining armor, you quickly weaken the connection with them and risk losing their interest. No one wants someone else to be the hero in their movie. Let them be that hero.

Your messaging should be around: "We understand your problem, we see your challenges, and we believe you can fix it." At this point, you can take the opportunity to extend a helping hand to guide them along their path to success.

The first step to being an effective guide is to demonstrate that you fully empathize with their problem. In our business, we let our potential Client-Partners know that, yes, marketing really is tough, it really is complicated, and we empathize with them that no one makes it easy. Make sure that your core customer knows you are meeting them where they are and that you fully understand their frustration and where they are coming from.

Once you truly connect with them, your customers must be reassured that they can trust you and that you are qualified to be their guide. This is when you need to establish your authority. Many businesses are losing out on potential sales because they miss this step or don't do it effectively. They miss out because they do not showcase their past work, expertise or client testimonials. We demonstrate our expertise by sharing that we've helped countless Client-Partners overcome their marketing challenges and achieve measurable results. If they want to learn more, we share case studies of before-and-after results from real Client-Partners we work with. Likewise, you should make it known how many people in the industry you've helped and the results that they've experienced. Let them know how long you've been in business, the credibility of you and your team, noteworthy credentials, licenses, certifications and whatever else applies to your industry and niche.

Remember Donald Miller's quote, "If you confuse, you lose"? One of the biggest problems when it comes to business websites is that they forget to tell their core customer what action they want them to take next. This is why Miller's book, *Building a StoryBrand*, recommends outlining a plan for your core customer. Using a plan in your marketing helps you set expectations with your core customer, almost like an up-front contract of what's to come once they contact you. Nobody is going to agree to go down any path with you unless you show them what the path looks like. However, at the same time, you need to be careful not to overwhelm them with information. There may be 17 steps involved in your program, process or solution, but that's way too much to communicate up front. You need to simplify your messaging in that first interaction.

Let's say your entire sales and rollout program is a 17-step process. If you try to over-communicate by sharing all 17 steps at once, it will only add to your core customer's confusion and will most likely cause analysis-paralysis, costing you the sale. Conversely, if your competitor who employs the same 17 steps markets their program as an easy three-step process, your core customer will be drawn to the perceived ease of working with them and direct their business to them instead.

The more simply you can explain the buying journey, the more customers you will attract. Your product or service could be far superior to your competitor, but if they can explain their process more simply, they will win more business than you, guaranteed. Make your process simple and easy to understand so your core customer will be eager to buy from you.

The rule of thumb is that you want to explain your process in a maximum of three to four steps.

In our case at Tulip Media Group, we have a variation of the following three-step process outlined on all our website landing pages:

1. Book a Free Consultation.
2. Receive Your Customized Plan.
3. Grow Your Business

It's that simple.

Presented this way, it makes it easy for a potential customer to say YES! Even though steps two and three may encompass 14 steps in total, they're being presented in a manner that is easy to understand and that will connect with far more people. As Miller puts it, you are about to lead your core customer across a river, and your only job at first is to show them the three or four stones sticking up above the water that you want them to step on. That's it.

Having a plan outlined also leads your core customer to the direct call to action you want them to take. Too often we see websites and other marketing materials missing a clear call to action, which means these businesses are missing out on potential customers.

Your call to action gives your core customer specific instructions on what you want them to do next. Our call to action, as an example, is to book a free consultation with one of our specialists. For you, it might be to make a purchase or to request a demonstration. Just make sure that you're specific on the next steps you want them to take. If you don't tell them what to do next, how can you expect them to do it?

Sometimes a potential customer is not ready to engage in your sales process and will not take the first step in your call to action. That's okay. In those cases, we recommend that you have another option for them to engage with your company. Something that provides both you and your prospect something of value.

Providing a free resource on your website for customers not ready to engage with you just yet can be a great solution. These resources—like an article, white paper, checklist, or coupon—offer value to your core customer and give you the opportunity to capture their email address in exchange. Getting their email gives you the opportunity to create value for them and build brand awareness for you through an email campaign. Make sure the content resonates with your core customer and provides value to them every step along the way. However, the ultimate goal with an email campaign is to entice the prospective customer to take that first step in your call to action.

When you manage to connect with a prospective core customer and engage with their emotions, they are more likely to want to take that next step down the path. They want to be directed by an expert guide who is there to help them succeed. Your core customer wants to follow your directions because they know it's good for them, so instruct them with simple steps and make them obvious.

Throughout your messaging, you want to be very clear on the benefits of working with you by listing out the positive changes and other things your core customer will gain by engaging with your business. However, you also want to communicate an inverse incentive for your core customer. What happens if they don't buy from you? List out the negative consequences of not working with you and what's at stake if they pass up the opportunity to engage with your guidance. Illustrate what that failure looks like and how your solution and guidance will help them avoid it.

At Tulip Media Group, we illustrate that not working with us will cause prospects to lose potential customers because their core customers won't be able to find them online. We communicate that they are going to waste money on marketing programs that don't work and end up spending way too much on sales teams that don't produce results. We relate that their business and their employees are not going to live up to the potential that they sorely deserve, and their competition will ultimately take market share away from them. Fortunately, all of these things can be solved with a tailored SMarketing strategy from Tulip Media Group.

As you close your message to your core customer, talk about how they will transform throughout the process of working with you. Contrast what your customer is feeling about themselves now, before they purchase your product or service, to how they will feel after they've engaged with you. Detail how they are going to be transformed from their current status to their future state.

These are the components of the BrandScript that you want to embody to truly understand and develop effective messaging for your core customer. After you understand exactly who it is you're going after, you can start engaging with them in a manner and language they can relate to throughout your selling process. This is where you can really gain influence over your potential customers and move them down your business development assembly line.

Chapter Six

Researching Your Industry And Competitors

"Research is creating new knowledge." — *Neil Armstrong*

Now that you've gone through the StoryBrand BrandScript framework and gained a deeper understanding of your core customer, you're ready to research your industry and competitors. The reason we want you to discover your core customer first is that, at the end of the day, real effective messaging needs to speak to your customer, not to your competitor. If you look first at what your competitors are doing, it can be tempting to just copy them. Instead, you should be hyperfocused on connecting with your core customers first. Only then should you be looking at what your competitors are doing to gain intel on how customers are finding them and to develop a strategy to attract those same customers to you more effectively.

If you simply copy what your competitors are doing in their sales and marketing, you also run the risk of adopting outdated strategies and being left behind in the marketplace. If your business is not staying current and innovating with trends and online digital marketing tactics, then it becomes very difficult to attract new customers and maintain a profitable business model.

Most companies have a go-to forum or industry blog they always look to for resources and information. We highly recommend you do the same because it's a great opportunity to "listen" to your market and gain some insight on industry trends. For example, we love scouring Hubspot and the vast resources they provide to marketers like us. They are consistently providing free reports that outline upcoming trends for our business and ways to reach various demographics.

When researching your industry and trends, be careful not to implement everything you see. You don't want your focus and initiatives to be pulled in too many directions. Focus instead on the initiatives that will have the greatest impact for your company. Always keep your primary business goals and objectives top-of-mind and consider how you might strategically apply the information you find in alignment with your business model.

Once you are familiar with what's going on in your industry, then you can dive into how potential customers are finding your competitors. To do this, we assemble a competitive analysis for all new Client-Partners. For us, it's an important step because it helps us discover keywords and phrases that potential customers are using to buy from our Client-Partners' competitors. These keywords are valuable assets that can be applied to optimize our Client-Partners' website and blog for search engines, social platforms and pay-per-click advertising.

If your customers are finding your competitors online, which most of them are, scour Google, social media, and industry websites to see where your competitors are reaching them and in what format. To build an effective digital marketing strategy, you'll also need to know what customers are searching for when trying to find you and your competitors.

To accomplish this, you can use an online platform to perform a competitive analysis. There are many online platforms available, but one of our personal favorites is SEMrush (www.SEMrush.com). SEMrush is an excellent tool for learning more about how your competitors perform online compared to your business. It was created by a small group of search engine optimization and information technology specialists on a mission to make online competition fair and transparent for everyone. SEMrush offers insights such as traffic analytics, keyword research, site audits and more.

At Tulip Media, we use SEMrush to perform competitive analyses for ourselves and for our Client-Partners. The results of these analyses give us an understanding of our Client-Partners' industries and the opportunities they have to leverage specific keywords or keyword phrases when it comes to creating their messaging, content and pay-per-click campaigns.

Generally, when working with our Client-Partners, we ask them for the names and URLs of their two primary competitors and two companies they aspire to be like that are doing a great job in their marketing. Using SEMrush, we are able to pull data that tells us how many organic searches each URL received and how many paid searches they received from sources like Google and social media. We can also discern the number of backlinks to their website, which is where they received an inbound link from a third-party website. A growing number of backlinks shows increasing credibility and is great for your business if they are from reliable sources.

The capabilities of SEMRush don't stop there. It also provides statistics for branded searches versus nonbranded searches, which is what we are most interested in when we perform our own competitive analyses.

Branded searches occur when a user types a specific brand (e.g., "Tulip Media Group") into Google. Branded searches typically identify a company by name, and it's expected the company website will be shown on the first page of the search results.

Nonbranded searches, on the other hand, do not identify the company. An example of a nonbranded search would be typing something like "make a magazine" or "effective digital marketing" into Google and having a company web page pop up in the search results. The nonbranded keywords are what we're most interested in because they help us identify potential opportunities for our Client-Partners.

You're never going to compete with your competitors when the audience is searching for that company specifically. If someone does a search for your competitor by name, you are not going to outrank them on that search, nor should you want to. That person is looking for your competitor directly. They will most likely ignore your name appearing in the search results. That's why we focus on nonbranded searches.

For the best return on your digital marketing dollars, you want a strategy that will attract people searching for a nonbranded keyword phrase. These prospects are most likely searching for some kind of an answer or information but don't yet know where to find their solution. That's when you want to appear. As an example, if I'm an insurance agency, I want to rank high and attract those who are searching for "commercial insurance" in my marketplace. That's an example of a potentially strong keyword phrase.

We use nonbranded keyword phrases to our advantage. If we see that a specific search term or phrase is frequently ranking our Client-Partner's competitor higher and generating traffic for them, we zero in on the opportunity to compete for that search term and redirect some of that traffic to our Client-Partner's web pages instead.

Using SEMrush, we are able to pull a list of all our Client-Partner's competitors' nonbranded searches and see if there are any keywords or keyword phrases that our Client-Partners could be taking advantage of. Phrases that are deemed "low-hanging fruit" opportunities have good position rankings. This means that they are usually on the first page, they have a high search volume, they drive a lot of traffic to competitors, and they have a relatively lower competitive index for that phrase, i.e., there is not a huge amount of competition for it. If you use SEMRush in your own competitive analysis, note these as opportunities for your company to gain some traction.

One thing to keep in mind with search engine optimization and ranking well on Google is that it's a long-term strategy you have to keep working at. A single piece of content isn't going to get you on the first page of a Google search. You have to consistently and repetitively put out relevant messaging and content that is useful to your industry and keyword optimized if you want to outrank your competitors. Remember that you can't trick Google, so make sure your content is original and also of value. Not only does this help you rank higher but it also builds your credibility online.

Case Study
When we started rolling out our SMarketing programs, one of our Client-Partners came to us with the problem of being outranked by a competitor online. In this scenario,

they vaguely understood what their competitors were doing to achieve these rankings, but they didn't know how to achieve the same for themselves.

Our Client-Partner, Miller Insurance, knew their competitors were blogging and putting out a lot of consistent and repetitive content. As you'll learn in later chapters, this is the right approach to ranking in search engine results organically. Miller came to us to help them get a better understanding of how this competitor was receiving traffic and if there were any opportunities to compete for some of this traffic.

This is when we stepped in and performed a competitive analysis. Using SEMrush, we were able to "peer behind the curtain," see which keywords were getting the traffic for Miller's competitors, and advise them on ways they could start directing some of this traffic towards their own website.

Looking at low-competitive and high-competitive ranking keywords on Google, we helped Miller come up with a keyword strategy for their website and blog. This keyword strategy gives Miller a foundation to start producing messaging and content that is relative to their industry yet not very competitive for search engine rankings.

Now, Miller puts out content on a regular basis to build up their online presence and rank for keywords that matter to their audience.

Your final resource for researching your industry and competitors should be your customers. This is especially relevant for B2B businesses. Don't be afraid to ask your customers questions to get an idea of new industry trends you could address, things that are happening in their life or business that might provide opportunities or be relevant to other customers, and what your competitors are up to. The following are four conversation starters that you should be asking your customers regularly:

1. How is business going?
2. What's going on in your industry and market?
3. What are you hearing about our competitors?
4. How are we doing as a business, and how satisfied are you with our product/service?

The first question brings an understanding of your customer's current situation and highlights any pains and priorities they may have. It is often the case that what they are experiencing is similar to what other customers are experiencing. If resolving these issues is in alignment with your business model, it could present an opportunity to offer an innovative solution.

The second question acknowledges industry and market trends. Drawing connections between the first and second questions will shed light on how your customers are responding to changes in the market environment. It will also help you adapt your own business to stay current.

The third question is critical because it will eliminate any biases you have about your competitors. Ask your customers how they perceive your competitor and contrast this with your own preconceptions. Use these insights to shift your thinking to a more neutral standpoint. Some may not know how to answer this question and that's okay, but it is still worth asking.

Finally, ask your customers how you are doing. What do they think of your offerings versus those of your competitors? How can you do better? You can then take this feedback and really apply it to your business model to improve the customer experience, retain your clientele and attract new business.

Once you've finished adapting your approach based on your industry research and competitive analysis, you're ready to move on to the next step: developing and using an effective keyword strategy.

Chapter Seven

Developing A Keyword Strategy

"Don't find customers for your product. Find products for your customers."
— Seth Godin

If you've done your research and know which keywords and keyword phrases customers are using to find your competitors, it's time to take your strategy a step further. Now you are going to leverage that information to direct these customers to your own landing pages with a strong keyword strategy.

Developing a keyword strategy is often overlooked, but it is critical if you want to create an online marketing strategy that produces results. When a potential customer searches a term in Google, Google wants to point them to the relevant information quickly. When someone is browsing on social media, the platform wants to send them relevant ads and information that they will engage with. However, the only way the algorithms these platforms use can accomplish this is to leverage the information provided to them. That's what keyword-optimized content is. By executing a strong keyword strategy, you are providing search engines and social media platforms with the information they need to connect you to your target audience quickly and effectively.

If you are not strategically building an effective keyword strategy for your website, search engines will not be able to find you or they will index your content and what your company does incorrectly. This means they either won't send traffic to your web pages or they will send the wrong traffic. If you are advertising on social media platforms, you risk paying for ads to people that aren't at all interested in what you're selling.

The bottom line is that if you don't speak the language search engines and social media platforms need to effectively market your brand, their algorithms cannot help you. You need to make it easy for Google to rank you, make it easy for social media platforms to understand when to show your ads and make it easy for Google to promote your Google ads. That's why your entire digital marketing strategy starts with developing your effective keyword strategy.

Traffic that you receive from keyword searches is often the strongest and the most likely to convert on your website. These are visitors who are actively looking for information that is relevant to your business. In the short term, an effective keyword strategy helps you understand which keywords or keyword phrases are going to successfully compete for relevant searches in pay-per-click advertising campaigns. In the long term, you can use keyword-optimized content marketing—such as blogs—to rank organically in these same searches.

At Tulip Media, we use an effective keyword strategy to shape the way we speak in our blog content, social media posts, website messaging, landing pages, pay-per-click advertising and more to achieve real results. We know that consistency and repetition are key to achieving higher search engine rankings so we keep this in mind for everything that we publish online.

A side benefit to this is that staying consistent with our chosen keywords or keyword phrases in our advertising and throughout our web presence keeps us on point with what we want to say and who we want to say it to. In other words, it keeps us aligned with the marketing message we want to send to our core customer.

In developing your own keyword strategy, we highly recommend that you take advantage of a tool called Google Keyword Planner. If you are working with us through one of our programs, we will utilize this tool for you to ensure the best performance in all of your online advertising campaigns.

While SEMrush and the competitive analysis give you a look into what's working for your competitors and some opportunities you can take advantage of, Google Keyword Planner gives you insight into what your customers are actually searching for and where your money is best spent when it comes to executing a pay-per-click advertising campaign. The best part is that Google Keyword Planner is free. All you need is a Google Adwords account.

Think of your pay-per-click advertising campaigns like a car and your keywords like the fuel. You need effective keywords to make it easy for Google and social media platforms to understand your business and to keep your campaigns in motion. That's why developing a strong keyword strategy is so important. If you don't have high-performing keywords, or you're not leveraging search terms that people are actually looking for and are relevant to your business, then you're not going to have a successful campaign.

You can use Google Keyword Planner to search for volume trends, which tell you how many times a keyword is searched for on average on a monthly basis within the geographic area you're targeting. Performance forecasts give you an estimate of what the searches for that keyword will look like over time and the sidebar gives you various options to filter your results.

When you're looking at the results for each keyword, Google Keyword Planner will tell you how heavy the competition is for each keyword on a scale of low to medium to high. If a keyword has a low competitive rating, then it is returning a low number of advertisements relative to the number of searches. If a keyword has a high competitive rating, then it is returning a large number of advertisements relative to the number of searches. Be wary of campaigning for highly competitive keywords because you will be competing against numerous advertisers who may have substantially larger budgets than you. While these highly competitive keywords may be relevant to your business, they may cost you "an arm and a leg" every time someone clicks on your ad. In short, when more companies are competing for the same keyword or keyword phrase, the price per "click" increases. The last thing you want is one keyword eating up your entire Google Ad budget.

The competition index measures how competitive a keyword is numerically from 0 to 100. It's calculated by the number of ad slots filled divided by the total number of ad slots available. The lower the better because a lower number means fewer businesses are using that search term as a keyword in their advertising campaigns. In our own campaigns, ideally, we try to look for search terms with a competition index under 50.

Google Keyword Planner will also let you know the average bid for a pay-per-click ranking. If the average bid for a keyword is in the low range, you know the ranking for that keyword isn't in very high demand. Keywords with a low average bid often present opportunities to attract new customers at a fraction of the cost. Conversely, a high average bid means that a lot of businesses are competing to place for that keyword. Keywords with a high average bid can also present opportunities to attract new customers if your budget can accommodate the higher rates.

Once you understand what keywords your potential customers are searching for, you need to understand how they are searching for them. That's where keyword phrases come in. For example, we may know that there are thousands of people in our locale looking to publish a magazine, but that's just the "what." In order to capture that audience, we need to understand the language they are using when they make that search online. That's the "how." Some people might be searching explicitly for "how to publish a magazine," but others might be typing in "how to make a magazine" or "how do I create my own custom magazine." How your customers are searching for you is just as important as their interest in finding you, and you need to account for this in your keyword strategy.

Based on what you're entering for your desired search term, Google Keyword Planner will give you recommendations for keyword phrases related to your keyword. These recommendations are variations of what customers are actively searching for. Make sure you pay close attention to these variations because new recommendations are responsive to changes in customer language and industry trends that you may not be aware of. That's really one of the biggest strengths of Google Keyword Planner. It will help take the terminology that you're using already to describe your products or services and give you suggestions on the wording and phrases that your market is actually using. Use it as a tool to update your industry jargon and give you suggestions for actual terms people are using, all the while giving you all the data you need, like search volumes, competition, etc. You should review recommendations each week and adapt your keyword strategy accordingly.

As an example, our Client-Partner Miller Insurance serves residential real estate developers, i.e., people who own and operate apartment buildings. Going through the keyword exercise, Miller considered their internal jargon which led them to what they thought was their critical keyword search term, "multi-unit residential insurance." After all, that's what they called that line of insurance services. However, when we put it through Keyword Planner, we learned that by changing the phrase to "landlord insurance," it opened up a whole new level of opportunity for them. The search phrase "landlord insurance" was searched 40 times more often and actually had less competition in their marketplace than "multi-unit residential insurance." It was a no-brainer for us to capture that as one of their keyword phrases in their strategy.

Note that if you use Google Keyword Planner, you will have many keyword and keyword phrase options available to you. This means you need to be thoughtful and strategic when you select the keywords and phrases you want to compete for in your content and Google Ads campaign platform. Sometimes you can leverage all of the keywords and keyword phrases you've uncovered as having potential, but other times you will need to narrow it down to what is actually feasible given your budget and the number of searches for each in your market.

You'll also want to make sure you aren't using keywords that are too ambiguous. We have seen Client-Partners time and time again elect to use keywords they think will work for them, but in reality, they don't because that keyword or phrase also means something else in the industry or in society in general. This often means paying for your ads to display in searches for an entirely different product or service. For example, if we just used the keyword "magazine," we would potentially be showcasing our ad to anyone that was looking for a magazine subscription, the definition of magazine, what a magazine looks like, etc. What a waste! To avoid this, perform a search for your keywords prior to executing campaigns to see what other results come up.

When you have screened your keywords and entered the ones you want to use in a Google Ads campaign, there will be three main classifications for you to choose from: broad match, phrase match, and exact match. You will have the option to select one of these for each keyword or keyword phrase in your campaign.

A broad match includes misspellings, related searches, and other relevant variations. We use the broad match classification when we want to reach the widest audience possible. However, this can backfire because the impressions you get from broad match keywords aren't very targeted, and that could mean you're paying for clicks from people who aren't really interested in what you have to offer.

Phrase match means your ad will only show up for a specific phrase or a close variation of that phrase. This classification lets you hone in on your intended audience more so than a broad match, but it isn't as restrictive as an exact match. At Tulip Media, we tend to use this classification most when creating ad campaigns.

Exact match is the most restrictive classification. If you set your keyword to this, your ad will only show when the exact keyword or a close variation of that term is searched. You will secure limited impressions this way but the ones you do get will most likely be from your target audience. This approach is valuable when you've carefully researched the language your core customer is using and feel confident that your keywords will be used expressly by them.

There is also what we call a negative keyword, which is often forgotten about. A negative keyword is a term related to your chosen keywords that you don't want your ad to appear for. We typically use this classification for terms that people other than your core customer are searching for. In other words, it leads to clicks on your ad that are highly unlikely to convert. For example, if you're a watch distributor that doesn't sell a certain brand of watch, you could input that brand as a negative keyword so that you're not wasting your budget on clicks for a product you don't carry.

As you develop your strategy further, you will be leveraging your competitive analysis from the previous chapter in addition to Google Keyword Planner. If performed with SEMrush, your competitive analysis will have given you insights for which keywords or phrases potential customers are using to find your competitors online. You can take advantage of these findings by competing against your competition on those keywords and phrases, intercepting their results and directing that traffic to your own landing pages.

To rank higher in search engines and capture traffic organically, we use what we call an anchor term. An anchor term is the phrase or keyword that you want to be known for in your industry. You can use the results of your competitive analysis to determine an anchor term that is a good fit for your business. One of our anchor terms at Tulip Media, for example, is "make a magazine." This is a keyword phrase with low competition and what we want to be known for across North America.

Another example comes from our many Client-Partners in the insurance industry. These companies all want to be known for the general search term "insurance" in their local marketplaces. However, we typically work with them to identify a more targeted anchor term that will work better for them. As an example, for some we'll use terms like "commercial insurance," "insurance agency," "insurance broker" or "insurance agent." We decide between these variations by leveraging Google Keyword Planner and considering the search volumes and competition for each of these terms. We do this research every time, because what might produce the best results in Minnesota may not work as well in New Jersey. Every market is different so make sure to do your research before selecting an anchor term for your company.

Once we decide on the anchor term, we use that keyword over and over on our Client-Partner's websites, their landing pages and their blogs. This is the term that Google recognizes as used most frequently and deems an area of expertise for the website. Once your website has been recognized as an expert by the Google bots, you will see your presence in the organic rankings rise dramatically. Over time, we and our Client-Partners have seen rankings move up remarkably because we've committed to using our anchor terms over and over again, becoming experts in the eyes of Google's algorithms and our respective target audiences.

Remember that unlike pay-per-click advertising, search engine optimization like this is a long-term game. Sprinkling your anchor term throughout your existing web pages will not automatically secure you a seat in the top Google rankings. This is something that you will need to work hard for and work towards in due time, using blog posts and the many other tools available to you. We have secured our rankings through keyword-optimized blog articles and being consistent and repetitive in our use of anchor terms on web pages for ourselves and for our Client-Partners. This is because we understand Google's algorithms, and we know this is the behavior that Google likes.

Once you have that anchor term established, you can begin to use what we call secondary terms. Secondary terms are loosely related to the anchor term and will be associated with your area of expertise by search engines and by search engine users. The secondary terms you choose should be searched for alongside your anchor term by your potential customers. This tells Google that the two terms are, indeed, related. Since you've already established yourself as an expert on the anchor term, also having content related to your secondary term will give you even more credibility.

Let's go back to the insurance example. Our Client-Partners leveraging "commercial insurance" as their anchor term may leverage secondary terms such as "cybersecurity," "restaurant insurance," "landlord insurance" or "business insurance" because these are terms loosely related to the anchor term, "commercial insurance," and will often be searched for alongside it. If our Client-Partners have a lot of content related to cybersecurity and anchor term "commercial insurance" plastered everywhere, then Google will determine they are not only a commercial insurance expert but probably a credible source of information on cybersecurity solutions as well.

Knowing which secondary keywords you want to leverage will give you something to shape your content around. Google Keyword Planner's suggested related terms can help you choose the most effective secondary keywords for your anchor term. You may also already have secondary keywords in mind based on your specific product or service offerings.

When you go to publish content online, use Google Keyword Planner to find out what the best choice of content would be given the current trends you just researched. You should always be writing about things that your customers have already indicated they are interested in knowing about.

Google has an advanced and highly intelligent algorithm in place for search results. It can detect content that is redundant or oversaturated with keywords. This means you need to write carefully and think critically about what your core customer is looking for. Produce content that is useful, relevant and written in language that will appeal to them.

We also recommend running your content through a search engine optimization assessment tool prior to posting. There are many free assessments online where you can copy and paste your blog article, title and other related information along with the keyword and keyword phrase you want to target, and it will rate your optimization effectiveness. One of our favorite assessment tools is www.seoreviewtools.com/content-analysis. This allows you to test your article for how well it will rank before you ever post it. It's easy to do and helps ensure your content will work for you.

To monitor the overall success of your keyword strategy, create an Excel "keyword cheat sheet" to keep track of the keywords you've found and the statistics behind each one. This will help you track the performance of each keyword and compare the results of your pay-per-click campaigns and content marketing initiatives.

Once you have developed a keyword strategy, you need to optimize your landing pages to convert all of the new potential customers you're attracting. In the next chapter, we discuss how to do just that.

Chapter Eight

Optimizing
Your Website

"Your website should be your calling card, or your business front door."
– James Schramko

In developing your new business development assembly line, optimizing your website is the most critical step because it will produce a greater return on your investment than anything else you'll learn about in this book. However, because of their lack of marketing strategy knowledge and understanding, many companies don't take the time to do it.

Having an effective keyword strategy in place and driving lots of traffic to your website is all for naught if your website cannot convert your core customer. Unfortunately, most digital marketers don't get this. They tweak some digital ads, create content, drive lots of traffic to your website and consider that a win. Don't let that be you.

Before you ever dive deeper into creating content and pay-per-click ads, you need to optimize your website for conversions by adapting your messaging, aesthetics and usability. You can do this by applying the messaging you've developed to engage with your core customer, the knowledge you've gained about your industry and your competitors, and your business development assembly line approach. We'll also look at keyword integration and page speed to increase your organic exposure on search engines.

Landing pages on your website are the most valuable tool you can use to capture prospects and drive conversions. In plain English, what we mean is this: a landing page—the page a potential customer "lands" on—is a specific page on your website where people are sent to from your pay-per-click ads, your social media or directed to from your blog articles. A landing page converts qualified visitors by directing them to take action. You can use landing pages to automate the first half of your business development assembly line by having qualified leads self-direct themselves into your sales process.

Depending on your mix of products or service offerings, you may need more than one landing page on your website. The general rule of thumb is that you will most likely need one landing page for each major customer segment that you serve. For example, our Client-Partners in the insurance space most often need two landing pages: one for their commercial clients and one for their personal insurance customers.

If you need only one landing page, it would most likely become the homepage of your website. If you require more than one landing page, they may be non-parent pages. This way, visitors can't easily navigate to those pages directly from your homepage.

To do this effectively, you need to make sure your landing pages are prepared to receive traffic and formatted in a way that will speak to your core customer so they convert and take the action you want them to take.

The metaphor we like to use here is that you need to prepare your storefront for success before you start attracting people to it. In a physical storefront, you would make sure your store was clean and vibrant before opening. You would also ensure that your shelves were stocked, full of products for customers to buy and merchandised well. Can you imagine walking into a store that appeared dirty and disorganized and didn't inspire a good shopping experience? How would you feel about shopping there? The same idea applies to the environment you create for your customers online.

However, most digital marketers don't think about that. They only worry about driving traffic to your site. This would be the same as a marketer driving people to your store only to find it very difficult to shop in. For this reason, you are simply wasting your time and money if you start attracting people to your "storefront," or your website, before you are ready for them.

Having keyword-optimized ads and content can only take you so far if your potential customers don't feel their needs are being met when they land on your web page. If they don't like what they see or can't easily find what they're looking for, they'll simply leave and you'll be left with a wasted click and a missed sales opportunity. Knowing what you know now about your core customer, you have the power to provide them with exactly what they need when they land on your site.

Optimizing your landing pages for conversions starts with your messaging. On every landing page, you will be leveraging content to meet the customers where they are and give them the solution to the problem they've been researching. However, your messaging needs to be formatted in a very specific way when you are engaging with potential customers online.

Remember StoryBrand and your BrandScript from Chapter Five? Your website is the perfect place to use that messaging that you developed when you created your own BrandScript. One test you can do quickly on your website that was also created by Donald Miller is called the "grunt" test.

The grunt test recognizes the human brain's natural instinct is to "survive and thrive," meaning it will filter out any information it feels is unnecessary or confusing. To satisfy the grunt test, your messaging should directly and boldly answer three simple questions for your target customer, filtering out the unnecessary and the confusing before they do. When you've satisfied the test, your customer should grunt in satisfaction that you have answered these three questions for them in under three seconds:

- What do you offer?
- How will it improve your customer's life?
- What is required to buy it?

To answer the first question, be clear on what your products and services are. Help your audience conserve mental calories trying to understand your message by making your messaging as simple as possible to read. It helps if you write at a grade seven level. If you make your audience work too hard at understanding what you're trying to say, you'll lose them. You should always take this into consideration when communicating in a written format.

For the second question, you will go back to your core customer analysis. What is the problem you're aiming to solve? How do your products and services solve this problem? There is your answer. Now you just need to communicate this to your core customer as clearly and concisely as possible in a language that they don't have to work to understand.

The last question is the essential call to action that will direct your customer toward conversion. Again, be very clear about the action you want them to take. There should be no uncertainty about what you want them to do or where you want them to go from your landing page. This is a critical step that a lot of businesses miss. Can you believe it? Many of us forget to tell customers how to buy from us. Remember that all of your landing pages need to have a direct call to action listed clearly on them and maybe even a transitional call to action for those who are not ready to take that first step.

Answering these questions may seem simple, but as your selection of products and services expands, it can get complicated very quickly. You should be revisiting the grunt test on a monthly basis to ensure your landing pages still satisfy all three points without overwhelming potential customers.

You also need to make sure all the information you want your visitors to know is "above the fold," i.e., appearing on your customer's screen before they start scrolling. All of the information necessary to satisfy the grunt test, especially, should be located above the fold if you want to secure any type of engagement so that you have a chance for a conversion.

When potential customers land on your page, will they know exactly what your company does and what action you want them to take right away?

Whether your call to action is to book an introductory call, schedule a free consultation, make an appointment for a product demonstration or simply download a free resource, it should be clear to them as soon as the page loads on their screen.

If you're unsure, go onto your landing page as a customer who knows nothing about your company and see if you feel satisfied that the three questions above have been answered within those first few seconds of landing on that page. Is everything clear, concise and to the point? If not, make adjustments until the answer is yes. If your customer gets confused, they are more likely to abandon your page than to work and burn unnecessary mental calories to figure out what you do and the next step you want them to take. Don't lose them.

Finally, does each landing page have messaging that is cohesive with your keyword strategy? In other words, does the page content align with what potential customers are actually searching for? Does the content contain the keyword or keyword phrase they are actually using? The last thing you want to do is have someone who is looking for your product or service click on your ad, which you pay for, and then lose them because your website's messaging is not aligned with what you are advertising. Not only did you waste your money on the click but you also wasted the visitor's time because your messaging wasn't clear and they got confused.

Remember to always put yourself in your customer's shoes and speak to them where they are at. Use vocabulary that's simple and straight to the point on all of your landing pages and produce content with their perspective in mind. If you don't do this, you simply won't be communicating effectively with them.

Once you've modified your messaging, move on to an assessment of your landing page aesthetics. If you already have branding guidelines, then you can easily apply these to your landing pages or have your web developer do so. If you don't, draw on your knowledge of your industry and competitors to formulate a design that will appeal to your core customer. Determine if your landing pages showcase the problems your potential customers are having and attractively display your products and services as viable solutions to these problems. At this point, you may recruit a designer to help you.

As you move through the design process, pay special attention to the layout of your landing pages. The layout you choose should be optimized for both desktop and mobile visitors, boldly displaying everything you want your customers to see right away above the fold on every screen.

Case Study

Back in early January of 2020, we were getting tons of traffic to a landing page from a Google ad we were running, but we weren't getting the conversions we were expecting. This was puzzling Jessica greatly. What she came to realize was that the landing page—built before she had come back from maternity leave—had been designed for the eyes of people on their desktop computers. Conversely, the traffic from the Google ad was 90 percent mobile users. When the users were directed to the landing page on mobile, the first thing they were seeing was not necessarily related to the ad they had clicked on.

On desktop, our landing page showcased our services for both magazine and newsletter publishing. On mobile, the landing page would show newsletter publishing first. This meant that if the user clicked on an ad for custom magazine publishing, which was the most popular search term, they would become confused when they landed on promotional material for newsletter publishing. Because of this flaw in our page layout, we were foregoing conversions with many mobile users.

What Jessica did to resolve this was switch the order of our promotional material so that magazine publishing was showcased first. Just by making this small tweak, we went from receiving one inbound lead per week to one inbound lead per day. That's a sevenfold increase simply from changing the order of our services so that the right one could be seen "above the fold" on mobile.

As you're optimizing your landing pages or looking at them through the eyes of your core customer, make sure you're also considering how these pages appear to your mobile visitors. Nowadays, most people view web pages on their mobile phone or tablet, which displays very differently from a desktop computer. If you don't optimize your website and landing pages for both mobile and desktop, you're likely going to push your bounce rate up, leaving a trail of unnecessarily missed conversions.

Keep in mind when you're optimizing your landing page aesthetics that you aren't just trying to make it look pretty. Aesthetics are important in the customer journey, but the messaging is still more important to optimize for discovery and engagement. Making sure your customers can find you and will convert comes first.

Circle back to your keyword strategy and leverage appropriate keywords on all of your landing pages. Assign every page a meta description and header and each image an alternate text. Google is not able to read images, so having alternative text on your images further optimizes your landing pages for search engine discovery and ranking. Your meta descriptions, headers, and alternate texts should all be search-engine-optimized as well. Remember, consistency and repetition are key.

Another thing to consider when optimizing your landing pages is to ensure they are built for speed. Your page speed has a severe impact on your placement in search engine results. If your landing page loads slowly, this tells Google that it isn't very usable and significantly reduces your ranking. Your web developer can help you achieve high speed in the back end by decreasing the number of functions your website relies on and eliminating redundant lines of communication.

Case Study

One of our Client-Partners made the grave error of building a website solely for aesthetic purposes without considering the importance of search engine optimization. This company sunk nearly $50,000 into a stunning website that just did not place on the search engines. After having a conversation with them and realizing what had happened, we encouraged them to approach the company that had designed the website.

Unfortunately, the designer refuted any design flaws by saying the company had asked for an attractive website, not one intended for ranking or blogging.

Fortunately, we were able to help them get their blog up and running with search engine optimized content. Jessica also consulted on their website's back end and developed meta descriptions, targeted headers and an effective keyword strategy. We performed a competitive analysis and also gave them tips on alternate texts and some WordPress plugins like the All in One SEO (AIOSEO) and the Yoast tool. Since optimizing each page, they are now ranking much stronger on Google.

This just goes to show how important it is to understand the purpose of your web pages so that you don't get yourself into a similar situation. Always take a multifaceted approach to optimization and ensure that you address all points. It takes a lot of time and hard work, but the results will be worth it and you'll see your business potential grow exponentially because of it.

If you're happy with your messaging, aesthetics, keyword integration and page speed, consider now the usability of your landing pages. Above all, your customers are looking for convenience. In order to capture those sales, you'll need to have a seamless conversion process integrated into your landing pages. If you can create landing pages that have clear and impactful messaging that are also easy for your visitors to purchase from, you win.

Automating your online conversions streamlines your business development assembly line and saves time for both you and your customer. You won't have to worry about spending labor hours for prospects that don't convert, and potential customers won't have to wait on hold or navigate a phone tree for a sales representative to be available. Instead, they will have instant access to information and demonstrations at the click of a button. This is what we'll talk about in the next chapter.

Chapter Nine

Automating Your Conversion Strategy

"A website without conversion rate optimization is like a car with no wheels
— it will take you nowhere." – Jeremy Abel

Automating your conversion strategy by leveraging online tools and tactics is key to driving down your cost of acquisition. In fact, this is at the heart of everything we do in our digital marketing programs here at Tulip Media Group. Just like the stations of Henry Ford's automobile assembly line were eventually replaced with robots, leveraging automation in your business development assembly line fills your funnel in a way that's easy and efficient. For us at Tulip Media Group, conversions are the true measure of success in marketing.

We define conversions in marketing as every time a potential customer raises their hand and reaches out to buy from you or learn more about the products or services you sell. A potential customer converts when they make a purchase online, calls you to learn more about what you're selling, books a meeting with one of your salespeople or fills out a contact form.

Unlike most digital marketers, we measure success by the number of conversions that your marketing achieves. Of course we still pay close attention to social media engagement, click rates on emails, online traffic to your website and more, but we view these instead as various levers to pull to achieve real results. Facebook likes and website traffic are nice, but they don't pay the bills. Conversions do.

At Tulip Media Group, our goal is to achieve 10 conversions a week from our digital marketing. This means that if we are successful, we have at least 10 qualified leads reach out to us to learn more about what we're selling each week. When done right, these leads actually come to us as more than just leads, they come to us as opportunities. An opportunity for us means our prospect has met the criteria for becoming a Client-Partner before they reach out to us, so we know there is a high chance of selling to them.

Every business will be different. Ask yourself what you need to have in terms of new leads and opportunities coming into the business through automated marketing strategies to make a reasonable profit. Remember that you want to set your business up for success by lowering your cost of acquisition. At Tulip Media Group, we've successfully decreased our own cost of acquisition by over 90 percent in just 18 months.

When it comes to tracking conversions, there are many tools available to you. As an example, the easiest way to track conversions through your Google Ads account is to set up what we call tracking tags. Tracking tags are small pieces of code added to your website URL that provide in-depth analytics about the traffic you are receiving and about your users' behavior. Tags can be used for tracking scrolls, monitoring contact form submissions, remarketing, making calls or simply tracking how people arrive at your site. Your tags then send information back to Google Analytics and Google Ads so you can review it and adapt your strategy accordingly.

You can install your own tracking tags by inserting each tag's code, as provided by Google, into the corresponding line of HTML in the back end of the website. You can also use Google Tag Manager to do this, which is a little bit easier.

Once you have one tag installed, you can insert another on a second page to track the relationship between the pages. For instance, we use this feature to track how many users have moved from our "Book a Free Consultation" page to our "Thank You" page because this action clearly indicates we've made a conversion. We can also compare how many people have explored booking a consultation versus the number of people who completed their booking. Using these figures, we're able to assess what we call our success ratio.

Generating statistics for your online conversions is important because it gives you insight. Thanks to tracking tags, you can get a glimpse into the customer journey of everyone clicking on your ads, which helps you make decisions about your messaging and the way you present your products and services. You can start to ask questions and assess issues like "Why did they decide to click here instead of following the breadcrumbs we set out?" and "What could we do better?"

In your Google Ads account, you can track conversions in whatever manner makes sense for the structure of your business. Your approach may look similar to ours or it may be completely different. Think carefully about what each web page communicates to your core customer and the role each page plays in the customer journey, then use your assessment to strategically install tracking tags that will reflect conversion metrics you can use to grow.

Using Google Analytics, there are various metrics you can track to measure success. The metrics that you choose will be unique to your business and what success means for you. At Tulip Media Group, which pages are viewed the most, how long users spend on each one and what they clicked on to arrive on our landing page are all things we watch closely through our Google Analytics account. This is similar to examining the customer journey from the back end, but it also tells us what sources or mediums we're getting the most traffic from.

Sources and mediums refer to the outlets that are sending users to your website. For example, are you getting traffic from referrals or are you getting traffic from your own social media posts? Are you getting traffic from direct searches (someone searching your company's name), organic nonbranded searches or pay-per-click ads? All of this is valuable information when it comes to targeting your online campaigns and optimizing your landing pages to display what visitors are looking for.

Google Analytics also provides you with statistics like how long users are staying on your website, which pages they are visiting, the bounce rate, and other important information that helps you make decisions about the direction you should take your pay-per-click campaigns.

Once Google Analytics is set up and accurately supplying you with data on how people flow through your website, you should set daily or weekly goals for conversions. Follow up with these objectives weekly and adapt your landing pages and campaigns as needed.

After you have installed your tracking tags, determined conversion metrics and established your conversion goals, you're ready to start the process of automating your conversion strategy. At Tulip Media, we would prefer to spend time and engage with just 10 qualified opportunities a week versus 40 unqualified leads. The goal in automating your conversion strategy is to only spend your human resources on opportunities that are qualified and likely to turn into paying customers. This means automating your business development assembly line as much as possible to achieve this. Automating your conversion strategy means the prospects who do call you need to self-qualify before they engage with any of your people, freeing up your team to only handle prospects with real potential.

You can automate your conversion strategy using tools like ClickFunnels, Leadpages or your own landing pages, all of which can be highly effective. Most often we opt to take the route of using your own landing pages. This is often the best choice because you've already optimized your landing pages for conversions in the previous chapter. Plus, you are getting all the analytics and traffic under your own website and not a third-party page.

As you develop your automation process, think about your core customer, what their needs are, and how far they are willing to go to get the solution to their problem at each step along the way. If you ask too much too soon when attempting to qualify leads, you might lose them. However, if you ask too little throughout the process, then you risk wasting your time with weak leads that are not qualified. Think carefully about your process, whom you want to take action, and what you can do to encourage them. At the same time, you need to discourage those who are not qualified from moving further down the funnel and converting. This will require some critical thinking and very targeted messaging. We recommend reviewing your BrandScript to help you.

If your prospects need to speak with a salesperson before buying instead of simply filling out a form online, we recommend automating a scheduling process. This eliminates the time your salespeople spend answering calls and going back and forth by email trying to manually schedule a first call or product demonstration. By automating the scheduling process, it also increases your capacity to engage with your core customer in a meaningful way.

A scheduling service such as Calendly.com is extremely effective at automating the scheduling process. Your salespeople can control their calendars by setting up predetermined windows of availability. With Calendly.com, you have the option to integrate multiple calendars, connect with your teammates' calendars and distribute appointments based on everyone's availability. This service is especially compatible with administrative needs because it enables you to use customized parameters, such as having minimum scheduling notice to avoid last-minute meetings, buffers between meetings and limits on the number of meetings scheduled per day. Calendly.com is a very user-friendly and practical tool for automating any scheduling, and the fact that it can integrate into your website means prospects can book their first call or demo with your sales team easily and seamlessly online.

If you are a restaurant, other hospitality establishment or grocery store that normally takes reservations over the phone, you can automate your conversion strategy to save time and money. Platforms such as OpenTable are designed specifically for restaurants to take reservations online so no worker hours have to go into manually inputting this data into your systems. This service also helps you to build relationships with your customer base and store valuable data like contact information and preferences.

Social media is another important facet of your automated conversion strategy. Your social media pages all have built-in call to action buttons that customers can simply click to be directed to the landing page you want them to visit. You can also leverage calls to action on all of your social media posts by including links to relevant pages and blog posts. This increases traffic to your web pages and encourages prospects from these targeted platforms to self-qualify.

Don't be afraid to get creative with your automation strategy. You know your business better than anyone else does so feel free to implement new applications or processes you feel would be a good fit for your operations. New software and technologies are being released all the time in every industry. A little investment of time and money here goes a long way.

Chapter Ten

Filling Your
Sales Hopper

"I believe you have to be willing to be misunderstood if you're going to innovate." – Jeff Bezos

With your keyword strategy in effect, your landing pages optimized and your conversion strategy automated, you're now ready to start inviting potential customers onto your website and down your online sales funnel. We call this filling your hopper.

All of your work up to now has been similar to the first steps of opening a physical store. You started by stocking your shelves, hiring staff and making your store appealing to customers. These are all things you would do before inviting any customers into a physical store. Once you're ready to open, however, it's not as simple as opening your door and putting a sign on the sidewalk. Finding your customers online is really a matter of effective digital marketing.

When it comes to explaining digital marketing, we like to use the digital universe analogy. It helps to picture the digital universe as we do our own universe with the various web pages as planets.

If you look into the center of the digital universe, you will find the search engines that we all know so well. For the purposes of this discussion, let's paint Google as the sun around which the entire digital universe revolves. As we are writing this book, Google has 92.2 percent market share of all search engines.

Very close to the center of the digital universe are all of the mainstream social media sites like Facebook, LinkedIn, Instagram, TikTok and YouTube. These sites are near to the center, but they're not directly in the center. This is because not everyone uses all social media sites every day. Conversely, almost everyone uses a search engine daily.

Now, as much as you would like to believe that your website is close to the center as well, the reality is that your website is not located anywhere near the center of the digital universe. In fact, websites like yours and ours are located far away on the outskirts of the digital universe. This means that your customers aren't going to stumble upon your website, at least not on their own. It's going to take a little work to get them there.

For most of us, moving our website closer to the center of the digital universe would take a budget and a capacity that we just don't have. Therefore, we need to find another way. The solution is to execute an effective digital marketing strategy that targets your core customer and makes your website known to the people that matter to your business. Instead of moving yourself to the center of the digital universe, you will venture to the center of the digital universe, find your target audience and draw them out towards you.

When we think of our digital marketing strategy this way, we can look at the center of the digital universe as having two buckets. It is in these buckets that you will find your target audience. One bucket, directly in the center, contains Google and the other popular search engines. The second bucket, orbiting slightly off-center, contains all the social media sites.

The reason we look at search engines and social media as two separate buckets is because they require, in most cases, two different strategies to compete for attention. If you advertise in the search engine bucket, you'll target your audience through content marketing and pay-per-click ad campaigns that appear in search engine results. When you target your core customer through social media, you will need to gauge what they are looking for and strategically advertise on the platforms you know they are hanging out on.

Using search engines, you can attract people who are actively searching for something, seeking information from your area of expertise and trying to learn more. These are people who have made it known in the digital universe that they might be interested in your product (or at least in consuming related content). When you target your audience through search engines instead of social media, you're going to be interacting with this subset of people.

When you look to social media sites on the other hand, most often, users are not actively searching for your information. Most often, your audience is going to social media sites for entertainment, to keep up with their community or to stay current with the latest news in areas of interest to them. For this reason, reaching out to your audience via social media versus on a search engine can be tricky.

Depending on a number of factors, the right strategy for your business may encompass digital marketing through search engines, social media or a combination of both. When given a choice, based on your specific set of circumstances, we would much rather target people on search engines where possible. These people have already indicated their interest in solving a problem or obtaining an answer to a question and invested time into finding a solution. In other words, we know they are good candidates to become potential customers.

Meanwhile, people on social media are not necessarily searching for anything. Because of this, they cannot be approached in the same fashion. Quite often the approach you need to take in the social media bucket—which we'll talk about more in-depth in a couple of chapters—is to create great content that will engage your audience. Ultimately, the goal will be to get their attention and position yourself as a thought leader, drawing them out to your website to learn more.

You can do pay-per-click advertising on social media as well, which can be an effective way to reach your audience. When taking this approach, however, you need to keep in mind that utilizing social media for paid ad campaigns can be very similar to advertising on television or radio. To many potential customers, paid advertising on social platforms can seem like a modern day version of interruption-type ads.

When you're watching TV, you're doing so because you are engaged in the program you're viewing. Then, the advertisements come on roughly every eight minutes to interrupt you and to try to get your attention. Typically, this makes you feel irritated and unlikely to engage with the message the advertisement is sending.

Likewise, when you're on Facebook, LinkedIn, Instagram, or TikTok, you're there to engage with content, not advertisements. When the advertisements appear in your feed to capture your attention, it can feel like an interruption to the content that you came to see. Most of us don't turn to social media for solutions but rather for entertainment, engagement and learning. Even people on LinkedIn are there to stay current with their contacts and colleagues on a professional level. These people are not necessarily looking for solutions of any kind nor do they want to be advertised to.

This is why, in many ways, advertising on social media is the 21st century version of interruption marketing. However, the ability to hypertarget advertisements on social media makes it possible to position your ads as a source of value rather than an interruption. If a company delivers the right value-added message to the right audience at the right time, they can become part of a solution that a very specific segment of the audience requires.

Looking at it this way, depending on your company's product or service, social media marketing may or may not be ideal for communicating to your target audience. If you can't zero in on your core customer and provide content you know they will find useful without making it feel like they are being advertised to, then it likely won't be an effective tool. Whether or not you pursue your audience in this bucket is a strategic decision you need to make.

Back in that first bucket (Google), the dynamic is different because you're connecting with people who are actually in search of solutions or information. This means that by advertising here, you won't necessarily be interrupting what they are trying to do, you'll be taking part in it with them. If your messaging is on point and meets the potential customer where they are, you can successfully capture their attention. When done right, they will become engaged with your content and take action.

When you go into the center of the digital universe to attract people from Google, there are two ways to do it. One is through Google advertising, which is pay-per-click (PPC) advertising. Pay-per-click advertising is offered through most search engines, but Google will generally give you the best results since its algorithm is the most advanced and it is the most widely used. The second form is search engine optimization (SEO), which is achieved by leveraging content marketing.

Pay-per-click advertising can give you results almost instantly, but the quality of the audience may be lower and cost you more money. Effective content marketing results in higher Google rankings and, therefore, higher organic search engine traffic at a fraction of the cost. When you attract your audience through organic searches, it's also more credible and more effective than pay-per-click. However, it requires time and energy to develop usable, keyword-optimized content and have it move your website up the search rankings.

There is an ongoing debate over which strategy is better for attracting your core customer through Google: pay-per-click or content marketing. At Tulip Media Group, we believe there is a place for both strategies. What we do in our SMarketing programs is actively work between the two.

We use SEO strategies to create content for our Client-Partners' websites that will be indexed and found by Google. This makes it so people searching keywords related to solutions our Client-Partner provides will be better able to find their website through organic searches. Enabling those with questions or those who are looking for solutions to find our Client-Partners online through search engines is a very effective strategy. However, it takes time and work to get there, which is why we use it as a long-term approach.

To gain momentum in the short-term, we use pay-per-click campaigns. With pay-per-click ads, we typically see results very quickly, inside of just a few days. We've mastered this process by leveraging specific keywords to create distinct ad campaigns that get right in front of our Client-Partners' target audiences.

If you're just getting started, we recommend building a content marketing campaign first and making that a key component in achieving your long-term objectives. While that's ramping up, we do encourage a pay-per-click strategy to gain more immediate results. This will direct traffic onto your website where prospects can be converted into qualified opportunities and paying customers much more quickly.

In the next two chapters, we are going to dive deep into Google advertising and social media marketing strategies. Keep that digital universe model in mind and where your website and your audience fit in this model. Stay focused on traveling to the center of the digital universe, finding your audience in the buckets where they spend the most time and drawing them out to you.

Chapter Eleven

Attracting Visitors Through Google

"Stopping advertising to save money is like stopping your watch to save time." – Henry Ford

As you develop your digital marketing strategy and begin filling your sales hopper, you need to decide where exactly you want to focus your resources. You also need to understand how to do it. In this chapter, we're going to explore marketing in the search engine bucket with Google Ads, search engine optimization and leveraging content across multiple platforms.

Since you already know what your core customer is searching for and you have these keywords integrated into your landing pages and website, you're in a strong position to take advantage of Google advertising. Setting up a Google Ads account is easy to do, and it's free. One of the reasons we like Google Ads is that it employs a pull strategy. This means it targets potential customers that are actively searching for a solution to the problem they are having. While we do leverage other forms of pay-per-click advertising on social media, it's our experience that Google provides a strong and consistent return on investment.

Many companies get stuck on all the options that come with having to create a Google ad. First, you need to choose the type of ads you want to run. These include display, search and smart ads. You also need to let Google know what you want your ad to do. This might be to get visitors to your website or to have potential customers call your business. That's just two. We know these decisions can quickly become overwhelming, so we're going to break it down for you.

Smart ads are a great starting point for beginners. This is where Google essentially makes an ad for you. However, while it may seem like a convenient option, it doesn't leverage all the keyword research and core customer development you've done. By using smart ads, you may miss out on opportunities to engage with your core customers because Google doesn't understand your keywords and keyword phrases, where to look for your core customers or the language they are using like you do. Running a search ad is a better option because you can optimize these ads to show on searches for keywords you know your core customers are using.

When you make a Google ad, you need to create headlines and descriptions for your landing page and provide a URL. In your headline, descriptions, and URL slug, make sure you include the keyword or keyword phrase you're targeting. You should also include an empathy statement to connect with your core customer, a value proposition (a statement of the value you'll provide to your customers) and of course your call to action.

Use your headlines to speak to the problem that your core customer is having. For example, if your customer doesn't know how to publish a magazine or newsletter, that is the problem your customer needs to solve. Headlines that speak to their problem would say something like "Publish Your Custom Magazine" or "Publish Your Quarterly Newsletter."

Your value proposition should also be relayed prominently in your headlines and leveraged in your descriptions. This will help you build credibility. Add further value with your call to action, pushing your targeted prospect to make that conversion.

If you select text ads for your campaign, Google will always show your ads based on the keywords you've provided. However, if you choose to use responsive ads for your search ad campaign, Google will use its algorithm to determine which headlines and descriptions in your roster are most appropriate for the user making the search. It bases this decision on other data it has collected on the user that you may not have access to, such as demographics, geographic markets and more. At Tulip Media, we use a combination of text and responsive ads depending on our Client-Partner and the SMarketing strategy we have in place.

You also need to consider those you don't want to attract. Make sure your ads are not only attracting qualified customers but also repelling those who are not qualified. This is why your messaging is so important and why we recommend you complete a BrandScript before starting any marketing campaign. Use language that connects with your audience and clearly conveys what you are offering in simple terms so only those looking for that specific opportunity will be drawn to click.

Pay-per-click advertising is a strategy that will start filling your hopper right away. However, it can be expensive to compete for popular search terms. Also, from your audience's standpoint, organic search results, or those search results that appear below the paid ads on Google, are deemed as more credible than paid search results. For this reason, traffic you gain to your website from pay-per-click advertising may not be as valuable as that gained from organic searches. That's where content marketing comes into play.

Referring to your competitive analysis and keyword strategy will give you ideas for the kind of content your audience is searching for, and therefore the kind of content you might want to create to engage them. You can leverage new content ideas for articles, videos, social media posts, podcasts or whatever content best suits your market from your keyword strategy. Remember that repetition and consistency are key when it comes to optimizing your content for search engines. The more you talk about your keywords and phrases, the more you're going to see those rankings increase over time.

Unlike pay-per-click advertising, seeing results with organic content marketing can take months. Remind yourself to be patient. Depending on your industry, you will see results in a few months to a year's time with effectively leveraged content and a carefully developed keyword strategy.

There are a few tricks to getting noticed faster. At Tulip Media, we call these tricks the "Behaviors That Google Likes." Some of these behaviors include setting up Google Search Console, getting an SEO plugin on your website, making your website mobile friendly and of course, consistent original content generation.

Google Search Console is a service available through Google that allows businesses to check the search engine index status and optimize the availability of their websites on search engines. Using Google Search Console, you can submit a sitemap and robots.txt, which Google's bots will crawl and return any errors they find with a list of potential solutions.

You'll also want to get a search engine optimization plugin for your website. This plugin will ensure that each page has one header and one meta description, clearly communicating the purpose of each page.

Try to earn or negotiate backlinks to your site with credible third parties. Backlinks are when third-party sites have a link to your website on their web pages. Backlinks create credibility with search engines and customers. If you are a B2B business, you might consider asking your customers to link to your website and offer to do the same in exchange. This will help you both rise faster.

Google will reward you when you optimize your website for loading speed, alternate image descriptions with keywords, shorter URLs with keywords, high security and consistent original content. You should also make sure your website is mobile friendly because up to 90 percent of visitors are now browsing from a mobile device.

These are just a few tips for boosting your Google ranking. You can find a comprehensive cheat sheet at the end of this chapter.

Case Study

An example of organic content marketing in action is the Englert case study found in Blurred. Englert Metal Roofing Solutions in New Jersey hired a candidate named Mitch Gaber to become their marketing director. Mitch decided one day that he would test out a new approach and start blogging about metal roofs on the company website. He was relentless in this approach and continued to produce keyword-optimized content every month over and over and over again. The keyword Mitch focused on was "metal roofing." He wanted Englert to rank on the first page when someone searched for metal roofing in the markets they served.

In time, the company significantly increased their ranking and website traffic. Over a six-year span, Mitch took organic search engine traffic from approximately 1,900 visitors per month to almost 15,000 visitors per month just by leveraging the company's blog page on their website with a thoughtful keyword strategy.

When Mitch left the company a few years later, the company stopped blogging, and in just 10 months, they lost 51 percent of their organic traffic. Six years of careful dedication drained away in less than a year. This reminds us that consistency and repetition are key to a successful and long-term content marketing strategy.

When you're working to increase your Google rankings, it's helpful to understand how Google works. Every time someone does a search online, Google's mission is to connect that search to the source with the best answer as quickly as possible. For this reason, Google relies on its algorithms to know which website has the best solution. If you want to rank higher, you need to demonstrate to Google's algorithms that you are the best source of information for that particular search.

The thing to remember is that Google's algorithms think and act very logically. As we already discussed, Google uses the language of keywords to understand what a piece of content is about. This is why leveraging strategic keywords and keyword phrases is so important. You need to take responsibility for letting Google know what your article is all about.

When Mitch at Englert Metal Roofing was posting blog articles, he made sure to leverage the keyword "metal roofing" in every post. He would do this by working "metal roofing" into the title and the first 100 words of every article. He then repeated it several times throughout the article, added it to the title of accompanying images (also known as "alt" image text), and finally used it in the URL slug where the blog was posted.

Mitch was also very consistent with his blog posts. He posted a new article every month without fail for six years. Google likes consistency. When Google's algorithms crawled Englert's website and saw that they were updating their site with keyword-optimized content each month, it demonstrated their website was current with relevant content. Then when someone in their market searched anything with the term "metal roofing" in it, Google knew Englert had a current website with a ton of information about "metal roofing" on it. Therefore, Englert ranked the highest for this search term. When Mitch left and the company stopped blogging, Englert's rankings took a nosedive because Google knew something was up. Their lack of activity could only mean that their content was not fresh and most likely no longer as relevant.

This is why consistency is so important. If you're planning to write 12 keyword-optimized blog posts this year, you're so much better off posting one a month for 12 months as opposed to writing 12 and posting them all in January. The former tells Google that your website is updated with fresh new content every month, so it must be relevant. The latter tells Google that, although there is quite a bit of content on this site, it's not updated regularly and, therefore, may not be as relevant as another site.

When you're writing articles for your website, keep in mind that every single article must be search engine optimized for a relevant keyword or keyword phrase. This is how you're going to draw traffic from Google, located in the center of the digital universe, out to your website. Every search term you leverage should be related to your anchor term and reiterate to Google that you are well versed in this area. The more credibility you gain with Google, the higher your search engine ranking will be.

There are many tools out there to use for this, but one that we like and use often is SEO Review Tool's content analysis (SEOreviewtool.com/contentanalysis). This tool invites you to input the keyword or anchor term you want to leverage into the software and then copy and paste your blog title and the article you want to analyze. It will then evaluate your content for the search term and return a rating of how well optimized it is for that keyword or keyword phrase. This enables you to test your article for SEO effectiveness before you ever post it. Our rule at Tulip Media Group is that no article is ever posted before it is tested for effectiveness. You should do the same.

We understand creating blog content can be intimidating and time consuming, so don't be afraid to hire a ghostwriter and outsource your content writing. You could even subscribe to a transcription app like Otter.ai, talk about the topic you want to write about, and then hire a writer to write the article for you. This is also a service we offer through Tulip Media Group because we recognize that most people running a business don't have the time to sit down and write an article for their blog every few weeks.

Over time, you'll accumulate heaps of content that you can also leverage through other various digital formats, spice up your social media and print for a long-term engagement strategy. At Tulip Media Group, we're big fans of repurposing content. We believe that if you're going to take the time to create an article, you might as well create a video from it, and maybe even a podcast or an infographic. You can also take all of the same information and put it into a printed newsletter or magazine to send out to your audience.

Now that you have a few ideas for what you need to do to reach your core customer through search engines and how to repurpose your optimized content, let's move on. In the next chapter, we'll dive into the second bucket—social media—and explore what an effective SMarketing strategy might look like using this medium.

The Google Cheat Sheet

- Get Google Search Console.
- Submit a sitemap and robots.txt (so Google can crawl) and fix website errors (get notifications/solutions to fix website crawling errors).
- Get a SEO plugin on your site
- Make sure that every page has one header (H1) and meta description.
- Don't have duplicate H1s.
- Request backlinks from credible third-party sites to help you create credibility with search engines.
- Make sure your website loads in under three seconds.
- Use alt text for images (also known as an image alt tag). Google can't read images, alt text tells it what the image contains.
- Integrate your keywords throughout your site.
- Use shorter URLs and avoid URLs with underscores.
- Be mobile friendly.
- Avoid having broken links on your site.
- Have a secure site (https://)
- Post **original** content consistently!

Chapter Twelve

Attracting Visitors Through Social Media

"Social media allows big companies to act small again" – Jay Baer

In the previous chapter, we talked about generating online traffic through that first bucket in the center of the digital universe, Google and other popular search engines. In this chapter, we're going to shift our focus to attracting traffic through the second bucket, social media. Note that generating traffic through social media is such a large topic that entire books have been written about it. For the purpose of this book, and this chapter, we're going to boil it down and give you the highlights of our higher-level strategy when it comes to social media marketing.

We talked briefly before about leveraging content across multiple platforms and repurposing it on multiple formats. One of the most popular ways to achieve this is to post repurposed content to your social media pages such as Facebook, Twitter, YouTube and LinkedIn. Your potential customers on social media will consume your content either by reading it, watching it or listening to it, so you will need to decide which of these media best suit your target audience before you post.

Your audience reads your content when you produce written posts, articles, white papers, and case studies. You can share all of these things on your social media pages. However, the best source of engaging written content for your social media pages and where you may want to host that content is your own website blog. This is simply because sharing your own content through social platforms this way will direct traffic straight back to your website. Depending on your social platform, you may also wish to post written content directly to your pages with backlinks that loop back to your website.

All of the written content you put out should end with a clear call to action. What do you want your audience to do as a result of reading this information? If you want them to make a purchase from you, direct them to do so. Maybe you want them to book a free consultation where you can tell them more about what you can do to help them. Whatever it is, make sure you direct them in plain English and don't miss this valuable opportunity to convert.

Another secret to attracting the attention of your target market is to use numbered headlines. Your audience likes to have a definitive expectation set for any material they are considering consuming. Headlines such as "Nine Ways to Look Good and Feel Better" will draw them in and give them the opportunity to quickly evaluate if this content is valuable. Articles in this format are also typically scannable and easier to read. Adding that element of definitive quantity to an already defined value proposition exponentially increases your chances of getting a click back to your blog.

Visual content is another popular medium for attracting your core customer. This is content that your audience can watch. We have consistently seen this medium expand over the last few years, especially since Tik Tok joined the social media bucket. We know we aren't the only ones who have found ourselves sucked into a video "fog" of continuous scrolling, when in fact we were originally just planning to watch one video. Your potential customers likely find themselves having the same experience.

Depending on your demographic, platform and the types of video content you are looking to produce, the length of your video is important. Keep in mind that viewers typically have a short attention span, so if you want to engage with them, you need to get to the point quickly. Some social media platforms account for this and only give you from five seconds to one minute of screen time per video.

Not all platforms limit video length, however. YouTube, LinkedIn and Facebook are excellent places to post longer video content. The more valuable and engaging your content is, the longer your video will hold the attention of your audience. Bear in mind, however, that in today's busy world, most of your potential customers simply do not have the time to watch a 10-minute video. Use your judgment, knowledge of your core customer, and assessment of prospect engagement to decide which length is most appropriate in your current strategy.

Have you decided video is a useful format for engaging your core customer but you're not sure where to get started with producing a video? Here are a few tips and resources.

If you are looking for high quality, a professional videographer can help you plan, shoot and edit videos to produce visually optimized content for your social media pages and website. A professional will work with you to capture the look and feel of your brand in high resolution and amplify the message you want to send to potential customers. However, if a professional falls outside of your budget, you can produce your videos in-house too.

At Tulip Media Group, we advocate for both approaches. For content that we're putting out for our target audience regularly—like a video blog (or "vlog")—we're big fans of producing videos in-house. Andy actively posts self-produced content like tips and updates to his LinkedIn and Facebook pages and receives an excellent response. We've found regular videos produced in-house to be more authentic and raw, and thus, they can be more engaging for our Client-Partners and prospects. Meanwhile, we reserve our core videos—like company or product profiles—for the professionals.

Creating videos in-house might sound overwhelming, but don't think that just because you're not using a professional videographer you need to do everything yourself. Freelance sites across the web have thousands of editors available to help you piece it all together. Check out sites like upwork.com and fiverr.com to find an endless pool of freelance talent to help you in your video production. There are also many sites, like Canva, that are easy to use and provide you with a template for short social media videos that are great for engagement.

One concern we hear about creating videos in-house is that our Client-Partners are afraid they will come off as too "amateur." To this we respond that being your authentic self on camera will, in many ways, actually give you more credibility because your audience will see that you are a real person. As for your actual video production quality, we do recommend investing in the right equipment, but the right equipment doesn't need to cost an arm and a leg.

There are three essential pieces of filming equipment that will wash your amateur quality worries away. The total investment needed for these three items can be as little as a few hundred dollars. To start filming high-quality videos in-house, all you'll need is a high-definition video webcam, a lapel microphone, and umbrella lighting (or a desktop light). Easy, right? Depending on your operating system, you may also need to download a recording application to record video.

That's it. That's all you need.

Now, before you start recording, think about who you're speaking to and what you want to say. You should always relay your message as if you're speaking directly to your core customer. Also bear in mind the action that you want the viewer to take as a result of watching your video. Make sure you keep them actively engaged throughout the content and include a clear call to action.

Video is the most engaging way to consume content, but it can be difficult for some customers to always offer their full attention. In contrast, audio content is content that your audience listens to. This makes it ideal for audiences that are balancing multiple tasks at once. Podcasts have become extremely popular in recent years because they are engaging and convenient to consume on the go. Anyone can listen to a podcast while they're exercising, driving or doing household chores. For this reason, creating a podcast to share content and promote your brand may be an excellent opportunity to connect with your core customer.

One of the most popular forms of podcasting is to interview others. You can pick the brains of experts or other interesting individuals related to your field and share their fresh perspective with your listeners. This creates a feel similar to a personalized radio show. Other podcasters take a different approach and speak to their listeners in the format of a one-way dialogue. This includes sharing your own knowledge with your audience, often revolving around a different theme each episode.

Perhaps you want to engage with your audience in a live, audio-only setting. In 2020, we saw the rise of a new social media platform called Clubhouse. Clubhouse is an audio-only social media app that allows you to join virtual rooms for live discussions, with opportunities for individuals to participate through speaking and listening. We jumped on the Clubhouse train in December 2020 for networking and also to speak with like-minded businesses interested in what we do. To this day, we get daily notifications from rooms we are a part of to join, listen, learn and network in.

Another way to engage your listeners through audio is by using a free recorded message. You can post your free recorded message on your social media pages or purchase a dedicated phone line for it to play along with a selection of consumer options.

The idea was first popularized by Joe Polish in his book *The Average Joe's Marketing Book* and the benefits are numerous. First, a free recorded message enables prospective customers to opt in or at least continue down your sales funnel without any initial labor on your part. It also eliminates anyone who isn't interested in what you have to sell without your sales team dedicating any worker hours to dealing with them. Recorded messages are relatively cheap and can be accessed 24 hours a day, even while you and your team are asleep. When Joe Polish first started using Twitter in 2009, he included a free recorded message and closed his first deal within a week.

Remember that everybody is different. Some people prefer listening to podcasts while others prefer watching quick videos or reading long-form articles. You have to know who your customers are so that you can speak to them through the social medium they enjoy and will relate to the most.

Client-Partners often ask us which medium is better. Our advice is to consider two things. First, you need to know whom your target audience is and how they prefer to consume content. If it's not clear to you, ask them. Take a sample of your existing customers and survey them. Let them know you're planning to start sharing more information about your area of expertise and ask them if they were to receive this content from you, what format would they prefer it in? At the same time, ask them what social platforms they frequent most often.

With that knowledge, the second consideration must be what format can you commit to. Regardless of the medium you choose to share content, it's only going to succeed if you are consistent. The only way to ensure it's consistent is to opt for a format that you enjoy and can provide easily.

Regardless of the medium or the platform where you wish to share your content, consistency is key. It's the only way this strategy works. After you start, don't get discouraged if after six or 12 months you are still struggling to build your audience. You have to stick with it if you want it to succeed.

A colleague of Andy's started a weekly podcast, producing a new episode every single week. After the first year and 52 episodes, he was discouraged and questioned his strategy after building an audience of only 367 subscribers. Encouraged to stick with it, he was excited to report that after his second year, and then over 100 episodes, he had amassed over 3,500 subscribers to his podcast. A full year after that, he was shocked to see his subscribers grow to over 30,000! That's a 10 times growth in his subscribers year over year.

Whatever type or combination of content you decide to produce, your target audience will ultimately be drawn toward your expertise and your ability to help them solve their problems. Make sure that all of the content you provide—whether it be written, visual or audio—is infused with information that is relevant and useful to your core customer. Never undervalue your own experiences and the attractiveness of your knowledge for your prospects.

Once you've decided the best medium or media for communicating with your potential customers, you need to decide where to find them on social media. In essence, you need to find your tribe and make strategic marketing decisions based on where they are hanging out. Where your target audience is hanging out will not only tell you where you should be posting your content but it can also tell you a lot about the type of content you should be posting.

For example, if your tribe spends a lot of their time on YouTube watching gardening videos, then not only do you know that you should be posting on YouTube but you can also see that it would be in your best interest to start a gardening-related channel fueled by video content. If you've found a lot of your tribe using Spotify to listen to podcasts, you might start digging into what search terms interest them and start a podcast related to these from your angle of expertise. If you know of dedicated Facebook or LinkedIn groups in your industry and locale, have a look into the way the members of those groups are consuming their content and start publishing that way.

Use the media you've chosen to deliver content that is engaging and consistent. Besides being consistent with your delivery, be repetitive in your message to your core customer so there is no uncertainty when it comes to what you offer and the action that you want your customers to take. That's how you'll succeed at attracting visitors through social media content.

Like digital marketing on Google, paid advertising strategies are also available on social media platforms. So far, we've covered some strategies for sharing content through social media with the aim of building an audience and generating website traffic. While this is a very valuable strategy, it is a longer-term game. If you want to augment your online traffic from social media in the short-term, you should also consider paid advertising on these platforms.

It's easy to spend thousands of dollars on social media advertising only to realize that you are not getting the return on investment you expected. This is because, like Google ads, advertising on social media platforms requires you to think strategically about your core customer and the value that your product and service brings to them.

When composing your social media advertising strategy, we want you ask yourself three questions:

1. What platform(s) is my core customer active on?
2. What is the main purpose or goal of my ad?
3. After clicking on my ad's call to action, is it easy for my core customers to engage or buy from me?

These three questions are a great foundation for building successful social media campaigns that achieve the results you are looking for. Once you establish your core customer's preferred social media platform(s), you need to think about the type of ad you want to create and your main goal for that ad. Are you creating a value/resource ad with the call to action being a coupon, free templates or a checklist in exchange for email addresses? Or is your ad's main goal to engage them and get them started in your sales funnel? Our recommendation is to try both awareness and sales campaigns to test what your core customer reacts best to.

If your core customer spends a fair amount of time on LinkedIn, then you are most likely going to see a higher return on investment with this platform. Knowing who your core customer is allows you to tailor your social ads using demographics, interests and audience targeting so that your ads are only shown to those prospects who meet your core customer's profile. Like Google ads, we recommend using your StoryBrand BrandScript to create messaging that is going to resonate with your core customer and solve the problem you know they are having.

The intent of a person on social media isn't to buy a product or service, nor is it to research a specific solution. Most people on social media are there for entertainment or information purposes. As such, your ads are often seen as an interruption. You need to be very aware of this when you're creating your social pay-per-click ad strategy.

Interruption marketing on social media and on your favorite television station are not one in the same, however. Unlike television advertising, social media platforms allow you to hypertarget your audience, drastically increasing your chances of engagement. This is a huge advantage over your favorite television station, which is broadcasting ad messages to the masses and only targeting through the programs on air.

Another major difference is that when you're advertising on social media, you are marketing on a platform that is conducive to instant engagement. When your target audience sees a television ad, they need to make a special effort to call the number on the screen or visit the website. When they see your ad on social media, they can engage with your company in just one click.

Between having the ability to hypertarget your audience and lead them to instant engagement through a clear call to action, social media advertising can produce significant returns for your company. You just need to make sure you do it right.

Chapter Thirteen

Engaging Your Audience With Print

"Content is King" – Bill Gates

Up until now, we've discussed strategies for finding your core customer using digital marketing tactics. At Tulip Media Group, we believe this is one of the simplest and most cost-effective approaches for reaching new clientele. With that said, when it comes to building total sales volumes, there are two other strategies that most often outperform all others. These strategies are engaging with existing customers to build long-term relationships with them and optimizing referrals from those existing customers. To do this, you'll need to engage with customers in a manner we haven't explored yet: print.

You'll agree the most effective way to fill a bucket is to first patch all the holes to stop any leaking. This same concept can be applied to your business growth strategy. Think of your customer base or your total sales as a bucket. To fill that bucket, or grow that bucket, you first need to patch any holes.

Customer retention plays a critical role in growing your business. When you lose a customer, for any reason, you need to first acquire a new one just to stay even. Then you have to find a second new customer to start growing again. If you retain your existing customers, every new customer you gain achieves net growth for your company.

As we all know, it is far cheaper and easier to keep an existing customer than it is to find and land a new one. However, we find it fascinating that customer retention is rarely addressed in business development and sales books.

Case Study

Andy had a friend who was struggling to grow his consulting business. His friend had several consultants working in his company and was serving dozens of clients across North America. However, the company had hit a roadblock in its growth and hadn't grown in several years. The service the firm offered wasn't the problem. It was world class and made a huge difference for its client base. The challenge was in the way that Andy's friend was approaching his business strategy and growth.

This friend was a firm believer that his services should be centered on short-term engagements, typically one to two years. Andy felt differently and shared with him that he had seen other consultants work with their clients in a similar capacity for four-to-six-year engagements. This led to a strategic discussion around his friend's business model. By simply changing the company's strategy and engaging specific marketing tactics to accommodate keeping clients for an average of five years, Andy's friend would patch his leaky sales bucket and start to see his business growth explode.

The number one way to grow your business is to first engage with your existing clients to increase the amount of business they do with you. To do this effectively, you'll need to not only deliver on the products or services as expected, but you'll also need to actively engage with them to keep your company top of mind.

Not only will high customer retention help grow your business by increasing your sales per customer but it will also optimize referrals because happy customers will be actively talking about your product or service to others. When a customer refers you to someone in their network, they are vouching for your company, spending their reputation to help you grow. That's why referrals are so valuable. The potential customer being referred to you intuitively understands their colleague is putting their reputation on the line in making the recommendation. Therefore, the potential customer will naturally place a much higher degree of value on their suggestion and will actually come to you half sold on your product or solution before they ever interact with anyone at your company.

The trick to retaining customers while simultaneously encouraging them to make these referrals is taking advantage of all of the marketing platforms available to you to engage with them. You want to consistently remind your customer base why they choose to do business with your company and why they should refer others to do the same. At Tulip Media Group, we are huge advocates for achieving this through print.

Many of our Client-Partners ask us, "Why print? In the modern digital era, why on earth would we put anything out for consumption in print form?" With seemingly everybody and everything going online, incorporating print into your marketing strategy may seem like an unnecessary cost. Why take on the extra hassle when you can easily transmit the same message online?

To this, we respond first with credibility. Naturally, anything found in print is more credible than anything found online. In fact, numerous studies have shown how content communicated through print is more believable and deemed of higher value.

There was a study conducted by Deloitte and Forbes a few years ago that found most audiences consider print content more desirable in general than digital content. The study, entitled "Digital is Growing, but Print is Not Dead," determined that roughly 50 percent of your potential audience is more likely to respond to print. In other words, if you only put out digital content, you are alienating half of your existing and potential customers.

If you're publishing content in the business genre specifically, the Deloitte-Forbes study found that 84 percent of customers would rather consume such content in print over a digital format. That means if your company is B2B, your content effectiveness will be discounted by 84 percent if you're leveraging only a digital marketing strategy.

Print, particularly for long-form content, is more digestible. It's actually common for receivers of digital content to print longer articles before consuming them. If they don't, the chances of going back to read the article later are extremely small. Think about the last time you saw an interesting article on Facebook or LinkedIn but didn't have time to read it right at that moment. How often have you gone back to read that article later? Sharing an article with your audience right there in the moment is the primary reason it's worth leveraging a digital strategy. However, it's very rare to go back to an article that's been shared with us digitally if we don't read it the moment it's received.

Conversely, when you find an article in a magazine that catches your eye, it's easy to set that article aside in a physical location where you know you'll be ready to access it later. If you get interrupted reading a magazine article halfway through, it's common practice to flip down the page to come back to that same spot when you have time to finish. You just can't do that as easily with an online article unless you print it.

Transferring your message to a print format engages your customers on a deeper level and gives the content longevity. When you receive quality content in print, it is more believable, more valuable and lasts a lot longer in your memory.

When we look at the shelf life of content, we see vast differences between the average shelf life for a piece of digital content versus print. A study conducted recently by Cloud Research showed the shelf life of digital content was less than an hour. In most cases, consumers either consumed it right there in the moment or it was never consumed.

That same content in a printed newsletter has a shelf life of approximately 14 days. In general, newsletters will be held onto and passed around for several days between people who value the information you're providing and want to share it with others. By distributing content in a print newsletter, you create something that will withstand the test of time far beyond the one-hour shelf life of a digital newsletter.

Contrast this further with a custom-printed magazine. With a magazine, you're not only delivering quality content but you're also delivering an element of entertainment value. The same study shows that magazines have a shelf life of approximately 26 days. In those 26 days, your magazine will be picked up, on average, by four to 15 different people.

When you create quality content and deliver it to your audience in a print format, it will not only have credibility but also longevity. Furthermore, you will engage your audience more deeply and set yourself apart from your competition. Print communicates to your customers and potential customers that you value them so much that you're willing to produce a physical resource for them to consume free of charge. These are just some of the reasons you see big companies like Costco or LinkedIn still publishing magazines and why at Tulip Media Group we are avid believers in leveraging both digital and print marketing. You can efficiently find new customers online with a digital marketing strategy, but incorporating print will enable you to patch holes in your business development and engage a higher proportion of your audience for the long term.

We've seen the results of print marketing first hand with our own quarterly magazine. We don't send out huge numbers of magazines. Our list of contacts amounts to only a few thousand names of people with whom we've been in contact or worked. However, it's a simple way of staying connected with those whose businesses we value and would like to keep in touch with. Receiving a high-quality magazine makes our Client-Partners of the past and present feel special and certainly beats another digital newsletter in their inbox. To date, it's been the single greatest form of marketing that we've done, bringing us more referrals than any other platform.

We optimize the distribution of our magazine by featuring our best Client-Partners on our front cover. Whether they've made a big move in the community or we just want to show off how far they've come with us at their side, one of our Client-Partners is the star of every issue of *Tulip Media Marketing Magazine* (*TMMarketing Magazine*). We refer to these as Client-Hero stories and encourage our Client-Partners to do the same by featuring their customers in their own custom print magazines or newsletters.

There's no better way to impress your customers than to talk about them in print. A blog feature is thoughtful, but investing in a print publication really speaks volumes about your ongoing relationship and your dedication to mutual success.

Ideally, you want to put an image of your featured customer on the cover and share it with their audience as well as yours. Our own approach is to do just that, and our Client-Partners are hugely honored to take part. We often send in a professional photographer to take photos of our Client-Heroes, and we use the same process when our own Client-Partners employ this tactic with their best customers. We then encourage our featured Client-Partner to share the piece with their friends, colleagues and others in their network.

Often, we'll even take it a step further and ask our featured Client-Partner for a mailing list of their top clients. This can amount to a few hundred or a few thousand contacts that we can then send our magazines to and share the press coverage that our Client-Partner received in it. Not only is this a way for our print to go viral, but it encourages referrals by our Client-Partner.

This approach works beautifully for securing new business. For almost every magazine that we send out, we receive a handful of referrals. When a satisfied Client-Partner refers us, or one of their contacts reaches out knowing that our Client-Partner is already doing business with us, the chances of us closing that sale increase exponentially. When you consider our cost per acquisition, this process alone most often pays for the publication!

By featuring your customers in your printed magazine or newsletter, you will gain their loyalty for the long term, optimize referrals from them and aptly demonstrate to existing and potential customers the amount of value you place on them. There's no better way to engage your audience.

Getting started with a print publication may seem overwhelming. It's one thing to write blog posts, but it's another to put out a printed publication. The best way to leverage print marketing easily and seamlessly is to repurpose your existing written content much like we did in the previous chapter.

The approach that we take with our Client-Partners is simple. When someone signs onto one of our full SMarketing programs, which includes both digital and print, we start leveraging a return on search engine optimization by creating content for them on a regular basis. We do this by way of keyword-optimized written content for their blogs. As we're doing those blog posts every month, we'll take some of the highest quality blog posts and weave them into a printed newsletter or magazine. We design it, lay it all out for them, bring in other guest contributors and look after the printing logistics and postal distribution. The majority of our guest contributions are secured through licensed content from thought leaders like Simon Sinek, Jim Collins and Pat Lencioni, recipes from Jamie Oliver and so much more. Because most of the magazine and newsletter content is already written, very little additional work is required to format it into a print publication for our Client-Partners.

This program is so easy to administer. If you choose to outsource to Tulip Media Group, we will take care of everything for you without you having to type a single word. Even where additional content is needed, we have a team of ghostwriters on call to do all of the heavy lifting content-wise, and a talented staff of editors, proofreaders, designers and marketers ready to put it all together and even send it all out through the postal system.

If you don't want to go through a marketing company like Tulip Media Group, that's fine. Take your best blog posts and bring them to a designer. An outsourced designer can format everything to look professional for print and appeal to your core customer. They can also coordinate with a local printer to have them printed into as many copies as you need, whether that be 200, 2,000, or 20,000. You can then work with the local post office for distribution.

It's that simple to have your own printed newsletter or magazine being published every quarter. With minimal additional time investment, you will have a long-lasting and deeply engaging publication that will keep the attention of your existing customers and effectively secure new referrals.

Chapter Fourteen

Getting
To YES!

"Get to be the best by practicing. Practice selling.
Do it three times a week for the rest of time." – Jack Daly

After engaging your prospect with an effective marketing strategy, the objective is to persuade them to take action of some sort. If your company sells inexpensive products online, this may mean they make a purchase. However, if your company sells larger-ticketed items or services, this may mean that they raise their hand to indicate they are interested in learning more about what you can do for them. These next two chapters are written for those companies who have this form of "online to offline" sales process.

In these cases, taking action may mean a core customer has submitted a contact form, called your office or booked a meeting on your calendar. Regardless, you struck a chord, captured their attention and got them to take action, essentially sinking your hook.

So, what do you do from here? Think of this as the manual component of the business development assembly line. You've landed an opportunity with your customer, but you can no longer rely on your automated processes to move them through the sales process. It's very similar to fishing, because up to this point, you set the bait and waited for the potential customer to bite. Now that you've sunk your hook, you need to take hold of the rod and put in the work to reel them in. From here, it's critical that you hold your customer's hand and interact with them directly to bring this sale to a close.

With the business development assembly line approach, your goal is ultimately to reduce customer friction throughout the entire selling process. It's critical that you make the entire sales process as smooth and as comfortable as possible for your customer. However, you also need to ensure a successful close. To do this, you'll want to make it consistent with their expectations. That's how you are going to get them to say YES! to the deal.

In Andy's first book, *How to Win Clients and Influence People*, he spoke at length about the three pillars of effective marketing: digital, print and interactive marketing. We've talked about digital and print marketing in the previous chapters, but we have yet to explore interactive marketing.

The steps in the selling process where you're first interacting with a prospect are still considered marketing to a great extent. This is because you're still in the process of securing your prospect's attention while reeling them into a verbal agreement. For this reason, it's important that whoever takes on those first communications uses sales messaging that reinforces your marketing messaging. This is what we call interactive marketing.

We often see companies initiate direct communication with prospects using a language and tone that is completely inconsistent with what attracted the prospect in the first place. These companies have highly effective marketing messaging to attract their core customer, but they fail to translate this messaging into the remainder of the selling process. When this happens, the business quickly loses credibility because prospects instinctually lose confidence in what is being said.

To avoid this situation, we highly recommend training your team to be consistent with your BrandScript all the way through the business development assembly line. Doing this effectively means that you will also need to update and train your people each time your messaging changes. This will align your interactive marketing messaging with the first half of your business development assembly line and give your customers confidence in what you are telling them.

Think of your selling team like a sports team. Sales guru and friend of Tulip Media Group Jack Daly always uses this analogy. If you look at the best sports teams, there is no way the coaches would allow their players to practice on game day. Daly is adamant that in order to sell successfully, your team needs to practice, practice, and practice some more prior to interacting with prospects. This way, when it's time to close a deal, your team is at their peak performance and ready to win the prospect over.

Daly's favorite tool to use is role practicing. He specifically distinguishes it from role playing because it's not playing and it should not be taken lightly. The way role practicing works is this: you bring three of your customer-facing people together and assign them each a role. One person acts as the seller, one as the prospect and one as the observer.

The idea is to practice an introductory or inbound phone call between the seller and the prospect with the observer standing by to provide feedback. Repeat the exercise three times so each person has a chance to fill each role. The observer should refer to the marketing messaging and assess the seller's performance for consistency. Based on the observer's feedback, each seller can improve their performance prior to actually interacting with a prospect.

Putting this into action on a regular basis will determine who on your team is strongest in interactive marketing. You can then use these people as role models and have your other customer-facing people "model the masters" as Daly puts it. This will further drive consistency in messaging.

To help prepare them for role practicing and selling, write out some talking points for your team that are aligned with your marketing messaging. This way, when they answer the phone, they can take cues as needed. Because we don't have a sales team in our company, we have talking points for our production team outlining what an initial free consultation call should look like.

When it comes to that first phone call, or whatever series of interactions you employ with prospects, you want to make sure you are very clear on what the flow of information should look like every step of the way. We refer to this as structuring. At Tulip Media Group, we have three different stages when we're engaging through interactive marketing and actually conversing with people. Each of these is structured very specifically.

In our first step, an introductory call, we take a 90/10 approach. During this call, we want the prospect to spend 90 percent of the time talking about their company and only 10 percent learning about our service offerings. So many companies waste time by telling a new prospect all about their company and what they offer the very first time they speak. Instead, it should be the exact opposite. Ask your prospect about their business, their objectives and their current problems (as they relate to the products and services you offer). When they're finished, you'll be in a far better position to present to them a solution that better aligns with their needs.

At Tulip Media Group, our first phone call is typically 30 minutes long. This comprises 25 minutes of asking about the prospect's business and only five minutes talking about how we can help them. In the first 25 minutes, we want to learn their goals in real dollar terms, how they are currently marketing and how much of a gap they expect between their sales goals and their current trajectory based on their current marketing strategies. Following the first 25 minutes learning about their business, if we feel that we can help, our reply is very simply stating that we can certainly help them close that gap. We then offer to recommend a solution that will help them achieve their specific growth goals and schedule a follow up demonstration in the coming day or two.

Taking what we learned about them in the first phone call, we know with much more clarity what to focus on and what gap in their marketing strategy we need to fill. We use this information to prepare an effective demonstration that we deliver over Zoom. The flow of information during the demonstration is more 50/50. We start off by reiterating where our potential Client-Partner is, where they want to go and what the gap is between the two. We then introduce the tailored program we've put together to help them overcome the gap and get to where they want to be.

The entire demonstration is a two-way conversation. We find it is most effective when we and the prospect each talk for roughly 50 percent of the time. When we do this, we leave the call with a polished, high-level program outline that everyone is aligned on.

The key takeaway is that it's not a one-way demo. It's a two-way conversation where we go back and forth with ideas and feedback, building and modifying a marketing strategy and planning as we go. This way, by the end of the conversation, they feel confident in what we've created for them and all of their questions have been answered. We use Google Slides or Prezi so that we can share that slideshow with them afterwards very easily. We also record the Zoom call so that we can share the recording if they have somebody else in the office who needs or wants to watch it. Our demos usually run about 30 to 60 minutes including the presentation and strategizing.

Once a demo is complete and we've strategized on the right customized solution for the prospect, we book a follow-up strategy Zoom call to review the plan, talk pricing and answer any specific questions they may have. The flow of this call is more of a 75/25 in their favor.

You can see that nowhere in our selling process is the flow of information more than 50 percent in our favor. This is critical for getting prospects to YES! because it's always got to be about them, their business and their needs. The more your prospect is talking and engaging in the conversation, regardless of the stage you're at in your selling process, the more value it gives the product or service that you're providing and the more it makes them want to acquire it.

As you are moving customers down your business development assembly line, don't forget that you are their guide. As we talked about earlier, they are Luke Skywalker and you are Yoda. This messaging needs to remain consistent throughout your interactive marketing.

Once a prospect comes through your automated system and onto the second half of your business development assembly line, they should always be moving. Remember that each station on your business development assembly line plays a critical role in winning the deal.

Getting your customers to YES! is a delicate process that needs to be carefully monitored and reinforced every day. By aligning your marketing messaging through all three pillars, treating your client-facing team like a sports team, focusing on your customer, structuring the flow of information at each stage and carefully tracking your prospects to keep them moving through the sales funnel, you will be ready to reel them in hook, line and sinker.

Once you've reeled your prospect in and received a verbal commitment from them to do business with you, you need to push them through to the final step: signing and onboarding.

Chapter Fifteen

Signing And Onboarding A New Customer

"*Personalization is what turns an ordinary gift into an extraordinary one.*"– *John Ruhlin*

At this stage, you've successfully moved your prospect through your business development assembly line and they've given you a verbal commitment to move forward. Now it's time to seal the deal and onboard them as a customer.

The first experiences that a customer has with your company set the tone for your relationship with them. Knowing this, there are a number of things you should keep in mind during this final stage. First of all, you want to ensure a seamless buying experience. In other words, you want it to be very easy for your customers to say yes and to execute on their purchase. Secondly, you really want to wow them and welcome them in a big way to demonstrate how much you value them. Finally, you need to set expectations.

These are the areas we often see companies miss when onboarding a new customer. Their buying experiences often become cumbersome right at the end, they don't "wow" their customers and they don't set expectations up front. These may not seem all that significant at a glance, but let us explain why each of these is so important to continued success.

Looking at the buying experience in your own company, what is your process like? What can a customer expect when signing on with you?

If you are an online retailer, how simple is your checkout process? If you are a service provider, how tedious is it for customers to sign your agreements? The reality is that complicated contracts and drawn-out checkout processes kill deals. So, how do you prevent this from happening in your business?

Eric Kish is the former CEO of Rompetrol, an oil and gas company headquartered in Bucharest, Romania. In his book *From 5 to 50 to 500: How to Build and Run Scalable Organizations*, Eric spoke about his experience turning Rompetrol around. From 1999 to 2009, the time that Eric was its CEO, he grew Rompetrol into a convenience store and fuel distribution network worth $3.6 billion.

His expansion strategy was simple, and it focused on land grabbing. For Eric and the Rompetrol team, land grabbing meant growing their operations by taking over existing convenience stores and gas stations, renovating them with Rompetrol branding, and using them to sell Rompetrol fuel. Eric knew that the first company to successfully do this would be the winner, and he was determined to make that winner Rompetrol.

One of the things that stood out most with Eric's approach was the simplicity of the contracts and signing process. Rompetrol's team was given complete freedom to structure a deal any way they wanted with very few terms and conditions. The only two conditions that Rompetrol required their acquisition team to work into every deal was that they had to 1) buy the convenience stores outright (no partnerships or licensing deals), and 2) they needed to be rebranded immediately as a Rompetrol gas station. That was it. Beyond that, the team was given a lot of latitude to accommodate the current owners' wishes and demands, and get the deal signed. Because of this frictionless approach, Rompetrol was successful in being the first oil and gas company to acquire hundreds of locations and establish its network.

Eric said there were contracts that were very formal and templated, and others that were entirely handwritten and faxed through to head office. Both were acceptable because, at the end of the day, what mattered was that they secured the sale and the location to distribute their fuel.

Everyone knew the two non-negotiable conditions to be included in every contract, and the rest was simple and up to the area managers and acquisition team to get across the line.

At Tulip Media Group, we've experienced for ourselves that complicated contracts kill deals. Our contracts were, admittedly, too complicated at one time and we were losing deals. We realized this and simplified our contracts a few years ago. We then simplified them further and further, and then we simplified them again.

It's always a balancing act. Of course, you want to give your customers enough information to feel secure in making the decision to buy from you and signing the agreement. However, if you give them all of the information at once, you run the risk of scaring them off. Like we mentioned earlier, if your competitor can communicate with customers more simply, they may well outcompete you even if your product or service is superior. The same goes for your signing process. If you overcomplicate things, you run the risk of losing the deal. The more complicated you make those final steps after your customer gives you the verbal okay to proceed with the purchase, the greater your drop-off rate is going to be. To successfully move your prospect through your sales process and across the finish line, your agreements, contracts, and checkout processes need to be as simple as possible.

Once a customer signs, the very next thing you need to do is wow them. Amazon provides a stellar example of this in action. In his book, *Working Backwards: Insights, Stories, and Secrets from Inside Amazon*, Colin Bryar talks about how when Amazon first launched, they would often give customers expedited shipping at no additional charge. The interesting part is that they offered this after the customer had already checked out and already opted to not pay the extra cost for expedited shipping. It gave the company a lot of goodwill and truly wowed customers, making them more likely to return and to make referrals. This played a huge role in setting Amazon apart in the early days. Wowing your customers means standing out in much the same way. What would make your customers feel superconfident they've made the right decision in choosing to do business with you? What's going to make them recommend you to their friends and colleagues? Figure out what your wow factor is and run with it.

At Tulip Media Group, we create and send each new Client-Partner a welcome package with a number of gifts that speak to our culture and the type of company that we are. This is our "wow" factor. John Ruhlin's book *Giftology* talks all about using a gifting practice as a business development strategy, and we've taken his work and philosophies to heart. John talks about gift-giving as being all about the customer, not you or your company. Bearing this in mind, our welcome packages have very little "Tulip Media" branded merchandise in them. Instead, our gifts are thoughtful sweets and treats with any personalized merchandise engraved with our new Client-Partner's logo, not ours. This includes etching our new Client-Partner's logo on the cover of the wooden box our welcome package is sent in. These gifts give our Client-Partners something to talk about and really make us stand out.

Lastly, you need to set realistic expectations with your customers from the start. One of the big things with onboarding a new customer (if you're selling anything complex at all) is taking necessary leadership and management techniques into the different stages of the relationship. At the beginning, you need to be highly directive. You need to set expectations on not only what you're going to deliver for them but also what you require from them to make the business relationship successful

Often, businesses are afraid to set expectations for their customers because they don't want to come across as demanding. However, if setting expectations helps you deliver superior value, then it's absolutely essential to do so during your onboarding process. Your customers are paying you to do a good job, and it's your responsibility to make that happen.

With our own SMarketing programs, a Client-Partner who buys into the full program may be eligible for our guarantee program. This is where we guarantee results for their digital marketing campaigns. However, if we're going to guarantee results, we need to make sure we deliver. In order for us to onboard and to deliver on a strategy that will work for them, we need these Client-Partners to be actively involved, especially during launch week. To ensure this, we have a very specific onboarding process.

When a new Client-Partner starts SMarketing with Tulip Media Group, we have a two-week onboarding process. It starts with some preliminary work and coordination that happens before launch week, mostly by email. This is when we lay out what they need to do and by when. Of course, we are there to guide them every step of the way. Part of the preliminary work is a pre-launch checklist, which includes getting all of their branding items together. For their website, we need access to their Google Analytics, their Adwords login, and their social media platforms. We have an involved four-step process to pair them up with the right ghostwriter for the content that we will be producing for them. Finally, we need their help to collect data for a competitive analysis.

For launch week, we require a commitment to a two-to-three hour Zoom call on day one to start the setup process for their new program. During that first Zoom call, we go through creating a BrandScript, discuss their competitive and keyword analysis, talk about their social media strategy, what the next steps are, answer a number of different questions and set expectations for both sides.

Over the next week as we're creating content for them, we get approvals and turnarounds very quickly because we set that expectation with them from the very beginning. If we didn't take that time to set expectations and make sure we have everything we need when we need it, we wouldn't be in a position to deliver our high-quality marketing programs and generate the results our Client-Partners expect from us as quickly as we do.

Things like fast response times, not missing deadlines and providing a highly communicative primary contact are all expectations we uphold in our company and we expect our Client-Partners to do the same. We can not guarantee results if they cannot commit to monthly tactical meetings and quarterly strategy meetings because we need these to provide a strong return on their investment.

We set those expectations up front because we are the experts and guides. Our Client-Partners come to us because they trust us and know that we know what we're doing when it comes to developing a marketing strategy that produces real results. This is something they cannot do themselves; therefore, they want to be led through the process. The same is true for your customers. If you need them to take certain actions in order to ensure your success for them, don't be afraid to set those expectations and embrace your role as their guide.

Even Yoda did not agree to guide Luke Skywalker without first gaining his commitment to do the necessary training to become the hero Jedi master and save the galaxy. If you need to ensure your customers' success, be very clear on what it is exactly that you need from them to deliver results and set those expectations early.

Chapter Sixteen

Continuous Improvement

"Continuous improvement is better than delayed perfection."
– Mark Twain

You're never done improving and your work is never done. No matter how far you come, there will always be an emerging trend or changes to the status quo that require you to rethink your approach. Embrace it.

At Tulip Media Group, one of our core values is **Embrace and Drive Change.** This plays heavily into our mentality to adapt and to always stay ahead of the curve. We're constantly absorbing new knowledge that can be applied to our programs to benefit our Client-Partners and we're firm believers that all businesses should do the same. Bring your expertise to the table, know your industry trends, understand what the latest technologies are and stay up to date with relevant current events if you want to stay ahead.

One thing we like to reference for ongoing improvement and development is the OODA loop. This model was invented by a military strategist in the US Air Force, Colonel John Boyd, to explain how to defeat opponents and emerge victorious in battle. As it turns out, it also has valuable applications in litigation, law enforcement and business.

OODA stands for Observe, Orient, Decide and Act. It's a four-step approach to decision making that accelerates the process of identifying a problem and implementing a solution. In business, we use the OODA loop to keep up with an ever-changing market. At Tulip Media Group, we apply the OODA methodology to everything we do including the ongoing development of your SMarketing strategy.

When applying the OODA methodology, you first observe by gathering as much information as you can from what is readily available at the moment. Notice that we didn't say gather as much information as possible. Instead, we urge people to gather as much information from what is readily available at the moment. If you wait too long to gather as much information as possible, you risk not acting quickly enough, which can be detrimental to your strategy. At Amazon, Jeff Bezos is adamant his team makes decisions when they feel they have 70 percent of the information available to them. He feels having more information than that does not significantly impact decisions and acting quickly offers far more benefits than it does risks.

Once you have made your observations, you then orient by analyzing the information you've collected, assessing where you're at and where you need to be. You want to fully understand the gap between your current situation and where you want your company to go. If you don't orient yourself, you can't make a sound decision.

After you've oriented yourself, you can then make a decision. This is when you develop a plan of action for getting from where you are to where you need to be. The quicker you make a decision, the quicker you can act and start moving forward.

Finally, you act by implementing the necessary changes immediately. The quicker you act, the quicker you'll start seeing results, learning from those results and improving your trajectory. This is essentially going through the OODA loop over and over again.

The goal is to move through the OODA loop as quickly as possible in a systematic way that keeps the process rolling. When Colonel Boyd used the OODA loop in battle, he commented that he would Observe, Orient, Decide and Act so quickly that he would defeat his opponent every time. Going through the entire process for the first time and attacking first, he was so quick that he would be moving through his second OODA loop— making his next decision and acting on his plan for his next attack—while his opponent was still trying to observe what just happened from the first attack. The more quickly you move through the steps, the more competitive you will be, consistently out-learning and out-pacing your competition.

Using the OODA loop will help you pivot when the need arises. This is an important aspect of continuous improvement. For example, when COVID happened, we quickly applied this methodology at Tulip Media. We observed that a lot of people were at home, realized that our current marketing program wasn't as applicable in this situation, reoriented our strategy and then decided to change our messaging to something that would appeal to the new needs of our core customer. Instead of continuing on with our standard messaging and scripted marketing plan for 2020, we adjusted our approach to reflect the new status quo.

As an example, we very quickly pivoted our marketing messaging to talk to our core customers who had suddenly lost all ability to meet new leads at trade shows and conferences. We targeted these companies with messaging that acknowledged losing a lifeline to potential new leads could be devastating for any business. However, there was another way. We could help them develop a digital marketing strategy that would enable them to keep their sales pipeline full by attracting leads online. Our marketing strategist would go through the OODA loop weekly to improve and adapt this messaging.

Pivoting your messaging and marketing tactics won't always be that substantial. In fact, it will typically just be small tweaks over time. Listen to what your core customer is looking for and make small changes based on what you've learned. Stay engaged with your industry and constantly seek new techniques to showcase your expertise. Whatever you do, just keep improving.

In your Google Ads account, you need to consistently tweak and optimize your campaigns to get better exposure and to advance your strategy. Your landing pages and even your website need to be constantly reassessed because trends change all the time and you're always learning new things. To stay in the game, you must be responsive. Pay attention to the data that appears every week in your Google Data Studio dashboards for valuable insights into what your core customer is looking for.

There is a famous story of Michael Dell at Dell Computers. During their period of high growth, his goal was simply to make the company one percent better every week. If his team were successful at making Dell Computers one percent better every week, they would be 52 percent better at the end of every year. That rate of growth over time translates into phenomenal success. In your own company, aim for that one percent improvement each and every week and you too will see massive growth over time.

As an experiment, start by making a small tweak each week. Making changes on a daily basis is counterproductive, but making a small change on a weekly basis will help you gauge your core customer's response to the new message you're sending out. Start by finding one thing you think you could improve on and adjust that. Assess the response, and if your stats improve, finalize the change and find another thing to adjust. If your stats suffer, review what you did and how it could have had a negative impact on your performance, then try an alternative adjustment.

We advise you to make a change or two once a week so that you can easily track what is working and what's not. If you notice a negative impact on your clicks or your conversion rate, you need to know exactly what change caused it so you can fix it. If you're making changes every single day, it becomes difficult to track which changes impacted your results.

Remember that quality and improvement come with trial and error, so don't be afraid to make mistakes. Focus instead on understanding your mistakes so you can learn from them and apply that knowledge to moving your business forward.

To keep everyone on the same page, sit down with your team each quarter to review changes and results along with your updated goals and opportunities. This is also the time to go over current opportunities and threats and to identify priorities you want to focus on in the next quarter. Observe the wording used on your website and throughout your marketing materials, making sure they are optimized for keywords and that your messaging is clear, concise and aligned with your BrandScript.

This is something that we do with all of our Client-Partners. We meet with them on a quarterly basis to make sure everything is going well with their program, learn about what's going on in their business and strategize on what marketing strategies will best serve them and their current business needs. Using this information, we map out their next quarter's marketing plan as it pertains to their website, their Google Ads campaigns, their content marketing plan and anything else we decide to integrate into their SMarketing strategy. At quarterly strategy meetings, everyone across the organization has the chance to discuss performance and go over what the objectives are for the following quarter.

We also recommend holding monthly tactical meetings. The purpose of these monthly tactical meetings is to have regular communication between everyone on your sales and marketing team. This gives everyone the opportunity to block and tackle the work that needs to be done and aligns everyone with the current strategy. Even if you are not planning to implement a SMarketing strategy right away, holding monthly meetings to build cohesion between your sales and marketing activities is essential to long-term growth.

Regardless of where your company is at, we've found with ourselves and with our Client-Partners that there is always something more to be done to stay ahead. Actively seek opportunities for learning and embracing change, hold yourself accountable and meet with your team frequently to discuss next steps. If you understand these things, then you're well prepared to execute on your strategy with your entire team aligned and producing results.

Chapter Seventeen

Company-Wide Integration

"Communication is your ticket to success, if you pay attention and learn to do it effectively."– Theo Gold

Now that you've rethought and optimized your business development assembly line, and you have a plan in place for keeping your sales and marketing ahead of the curve, you need to roll out the new plan with your team. You already recognize that having unique strengths at each station along your business development assembly line optimizes the highest pay time activities for each person and will maximize your return on investment. However, you need to consider how your team is going to respond to this new approach and plan your company-wide integration accordingly.

When Tulip Media Group rolled out our SMarketing strategy, we had major legacy challenges. First, we had a sales team that was simply not going to embrace our new process. We had decided to automate the first half of our business development assembly line, which meant that half the job of our sales team would now be performed with digital marketing tactics. We had then gone a step further in our strategic thinking and came to the conclusion that the best people to talk to prospects were not salespeople but team members who worked in production. This eliminated the need for our sales team completely.

Andy explained to the rest of the company that those who worked in production would be the best to sell our programs. After all, they were the ones most passionate about marketing and knew the process inside and out. They were the ones who could get potential Client-Partners excited about what we could do for them and ultimately work with them on a solution tailored to their needs and objectives. In speaking with a Production Manager or Marketing Specialist, prospects would approach each conversation with excitement and anticipation. This was a stark contrast to the defensiveness they displayed when talking with salespeople. Instead of "overcoming objections" like our salespeople, our production team would "strategize" about the prospect's customized solutions.

When we made this switch, it was incredible to see the change in dynamics between our team members and potential Client-Partners. This change in approach has forged trust with prospects and ultimately achieved the successful sales results we have today.

In our case, the transition was not an incremental change but a large-scale holistic change that we applied very quickly by ripping the Band-Aid off and laying the foundation for our new strategy in a single day. Our entire business model was pivoted and turned on its head. You may wish to take the same approach or you may wish to integrate your new processes more subtly. Whatever you choose, you need your team to adopt the new strategy, believe in it, and support it wholeheartedly every step along the way if you're going to succeed.

We would suggest doing it our way if the rollout of your SMarketing strategy is going to be blocked by people within the organization. If you believe that some or all of your existing sales team is going to welcome it and is willing to work with you towards achieving success with the new model, then there may not be a need for such drastic action. Keep in mind that, for those salespeople that stay, this will mean entirely new compensation models, revised job descriptions, new sales tactics and new ways of working together with others to close deals. If some or all of your team is ready to embrace these changes in the interest of the company as a whole, then great, let them be a part of the integration.

If your organization truly embraces the SMarketing process, the move to improve your overall business development strategy will be in the best interests of everyone. Making these changes will translate into more sales coming through the door at a lesser cost, sparking a very exciting time for your company as a whole. The way Andy described our new SMarketing approach to our team was that we were willing to blow up what was good in the pursuit of something great. It was a very difficult decision to make, but once it was made and we took that leap, we were fully committed to becoming something great.

Let's say you do make the decision to do a wholesale change like we did. Maybe you've realized your sales team really isn't producing the results you want and won't embrace a new strategy, forcing you to explore an entirely new approach. Maybe you're prepared to let any number of people go to accommodate this new SMarketing strategy, knowing that the only way to make it truly work is to move some people out of the equation.

Unfortunately, many of you will be in a situation similar to what we faced where the majority of the sales team is not at all receptive to such drastic changes. We knew we were not going to be able to make that transition without some real hardship. Our sales team was not willing to accept different compensation packages and potentially making much less money. Deep down, we knew that. Many were also unhappy with the introduction of automation because it took away a number of tasks they enjoyed doing themselves on a day-to-day basis.

Your sales team may not be the only ones averse to new processes. You'll also need to consider the changing mind-sets of the rest of your team. A business development assembly line approach to selling will mean less diversity in each role. Some of your team may enjoy working a variety of tasks and may not be receptive to focusing only on what they are best at. You should be prepared to address negative responses from some of your team and to let people go if they are not aligned with the new strategy.

Even if your team members are satisfied with working in roles that focus on their strengths, they are still going to be concerned with changing the entire selling process. Naturally, they are going to be nervous about trying something new and have some doubts about the implementation of this cohesive strategy.

Gauging the response of your team, you can choose to either roll the program out all at once or do it incrementally. In our case, it was best just to rip the Band-Aid off, so to speak, and implement all of the changes at the same time. If you are planning to let a large number of people go, this might be the way for you to go, too.

Alternatively, you may take the approach most of our Client-Partners have taken: integrating the SMarketing program into your existing business model and augmenting your existing go-to-market strategy with the new process. If you choose to do it this way, you will make the shift gradually, one piece at a time, so as not to muddy the waters too much at any given time. This is a good approach if you are planning to use most or all of the same people in your business development assembly line as you have working in your organization now.

If you take this approach, your people are going to be performing different tasks and new types of work. This can't be avoided. It doesn't necessarily mean that anyone has to leave, but it does mean that your team will need to be adaptable. When you roll out the program, you should start by having a one-on-one discussion with each member of your team. During this one-on-one, you'll want to explain the new strategy and process and where you see them fitting in based on their strengths and how they can best contribute.

Thanks to your new automated processes, many employees will be moving upstream and performing higher-level activities than they were before. This will most likely mean they receive a different compensation package as a result, and you need to be prepared to communicate this to them. You should really stress to them why you chose them to work in their new position, focusing on their strengths. Your execution plan for how you integrate your new strategy should be carefully thought out and presented to your team as a way to garner their buy-in and support.

What we have found is that when people are doing work that falls in line with their personality and what they're good at, pretty near 100 percent of the time, they're more satisfied with their work. Yes, you're asking them to do something different and that can be scary. However, you're also asking them to do work that they're good at, that suits their personality and that, most often, is what they enjoy doing most.

Look at it another way: you're asking your team to drop the parts of their work where they don't have the skills, that don't work with their personality or that they simply don't enjoy. In most cases, once it's explained this way and people get over their initial fear of the unknown, they more readily accept it. In time, the right people will enjoy the change and jump in wholeheartedly.

Your next task will be to educate your entire team. You want to get everyone together, including those who are not directly involved in business development as well as those who are. Take this opportunity to educate everyone on the changes you're making because they will impact everyone in your company, not just those involved in the selling process.

With more sales coming in, your production team needs to know what's happening and what the new customer expectations are. Your service delivery people need to understand what's happening on the front end so they can gauge what's going to be coming down the road and plan accordingly. Think about how your new business development assembly line will affect everyone on your team and make a point of addressing their concerns.

When you make any substantial change in a company, people often react instinctively based on their reptilian brain, which has been programmed for millions of years in humans for survival. For those who are most affected, or for those who don't handle change easily, they may fall into fight, flight or freeze mode. To circumvent this, you need to address those fears and concerns immediately and head on.

Immediately after explaining the new strategy, we recommend you start by answering the question that will be on everyone's mind: "What does this mean for my job?" When there's an elephant in the room, call it out. Put the elephant right on the table and announce that you're going to talk about it. It's amazing how small that elephant can get very, very quickly when you start discussing it.

Once you address your team's instinctual reaction and address their fears, everyone can then have a productive conversation about the new strategy. You can talk through it and help everyone understand that you are making changes for the betterment of the organization, ensuring the longevity of the company financially and providing job security for your team members in their new roles.

After you've started talking about the changes publicly with your team, you, as the leader, must be fully committed to implementing the changes. If you change your mind halfway through the rollout, it will create uncertainty and a lack of trust in your organization. It's okay to let your team know that, as you go down this path and learn new things, you may adjust the plan accordingly, but don't waver on the end goal.

We have witnessed countless initiatives that have failed because leadership was not fully committed to change. If you are not fully committed to your new SMarketing strategy change, your team will reject your plan and your company will fall back into its old habits. For this reason, you first need to be fully committed in your own mind before you start your company-wide integration. Make sure you are ready to communicate not only your new strategy but also your unwavering commitment to its successful execution. Don't sugarcoat this message. Communicate it with confidence, candidness and certainty.

Once you have successfully launched your new strategy, ongoing communication with your team is key. We cannot stress this enough. When you are in doubt, communicate, communicate and then communicate some more.

As you are making these changes, you will inevitably encounter many learning curves, obstacles and questions from everyone on your team. You need to ensure you are communicating consistently and that everyone is clear on what you have in mind. Any time you don't know the answer to a question, communicate that you don't know and that you will circle back on the topic with more clarity once you've gone a little further down this path and have the answers for them.

Acknowledge consistently that you value each person as an employee and that you want to work with them to find the right fit for them in your new business development assembly line. Ultimately, their new role will align with their strengths, their personality type and their interests. When you communicate these points regularly, worries and stresses subside, and soon you will find you have a team of advocates and cheerleaders eager to cheer each other on and lead your company to SMarketing success.

Chapter Eighteen

Final Thoughts

"Success is not final; failure is not fatal: it is the courage to continue that counts." – Winston Churchill

As has often been said, the definition of insanity is doing the same thing over and over and expecting different results. For nearly five years, we missed our sales targets time and time again because we kept taking the same traditional approach to sales and marketing. Looking back on that time, although we had worked hard to evolve our sales process, we were essentially using the same fundamental principles and getting nowhere.

As we covered in the introductory chapter, it wasn't until a good friend of Andy's, Patrick Condon, finally challenged him to destroy what was good in the pursuit of what is great, that things changed. It was Patrick's story and his strategy that inspired Andy to take action with his own company, action that eventually led to the theory behind SMarketing and the development of the process that we now roll out with our Client-Partners.

You don't need to be a digital marketing expert to start your own SMarketing initiative. You don't need to know everything or to have a complete plan. You also don't need to feel pressured to take such drastic action as Andy did. You simply need to start doing things differently.

We suggest you start by looking at your business development strategy through a different lens. Start looking at your selling process and redesigning it into a business development assembly line. Move your people around to fill jobs that they're best at or best suited for. Whether you have a team of 10 or 110, start by letting people play in their sweet spot, working in the area they are most effective and where they add the most value. Nine times out of 10, that's what they enjoy doing most, anyway. When you've done that, start to look at how you can automate things and enable your team to move upstream and perform more value-added work.

The important thing is that you start. Don't be afraid to take that first step before every i is dotted and every t is crossed. All the ideas and strategies in the world won't provide any value if you don't act on them. There's a saying that goes, "Execution eats strategy for lunch," and we believe this to be true. Yes, you want to plan, and yes, you want to prepare. However, those who win are those who err on the side of action. A person who's running down a path can always adjust the path as they go, but the person who refuses to act will get nowhere.

Know that no matter how prepared you are, your plan is going to change. That's how you stay ahead of the curve. As Mike Tyson said, "Everybody has a plan until they get punched in the face," and that's just as true in business. As soon as you start implementing any plan, face challenges, gain more clarity and see new opportunities, your plan will need to adapt. In fact, you may adjust your plan a hundred times, maybe more. Keep experimenting, keep responding to new trends and never stop improving.

Business is not a game where there's a beginning and an end, a winner and a loser. Business is a game that never ends, where you may be winning today and losing tomorrow. You may be going through hardship right now on the brink of bankruptcy and you may surge to become an industry leader next year. You just need to keep moving forward.

A final piece of advice is to find accountability from someone. We all need someone to hold us accountable if we want to keep advancing ourselves and our companies. Whether it's from within your company or outside, it doesn't matter. Hire a coach, hire an outsourced company, or find a colleague or a peer in business that is willing to hold you accountable for executing your new SMarketing strategy.

In our SMarketing programs, we take the majority of the work off our Client-Partners' plates, but they still need to do some of the work. We hold them accountable just as much as they do us. We all need accountability in our lives to make great things happen.

Maybe you're reading this and you don't feel like you're the right person to lead your new SMarketing strategy. Maybe you feel like your competencies can't make it work. That's fine. Just find a person who is. Find someone who is willing to take some or all of it on for you. You can always call us at Tulip Media Group for help. We'll give you some advice even if we never end up working together. If we can be of any assistance, even if it's just to talk for 30 minutes, we will gladly do that.

If you don't make a move, you're going to continue wasting money in your sales and marketing strategies. You're going to continue wasting opportunities for your company, your employees, your shareholders, your customers. Finally, you're going to continue losing customers to your competitors who are experimenting and exploring new avenues that you're not. We don't want to see that happen for you.

Mark Cuban once said that you want to wake up every day believing somebody else is waking up with the sole intention of putting you out of business. Whether you are running motivated or running scared, you need to be running. Otherwise, someone else in your industry is going to run you over until you are forced to do something about it. Today we challenge you to do something about it and proactively initiate the change you know needs to happen. Start running with SMarketing.

Chapter Nineteen

Bonus Resources

"We now accept the fact that learning is a lifelong process of keeping abreast of change. And the most pressing task is to teach people how to learn."
– Peter Drucker

At Tulip Media Group, we study, live and breathe marketing and business development, and we have been doing so for our entire existence. During that time, we have learned a lot. Our company culture is committed to **Embrace and Drive Change.** This means:

- We believe the sky's the limit. We ask "Why not?" instead of "Why?"
- We're always learning; that's what we do.
- We're continuously advancing ourselves, our knowledge and the skills we bring to Tulip Media.
- We're never satisfied and continuously seek opportunities for improvement.

In Andy's entire career as an entrepreneur and business coach, he's never seen another company embrace and drive change like our company has. We are always learning and trying something new.

Our employees have been a part of some of the most world-class learning events, including Scaling Up Summits, Genius Network Summits, Content Marketing World Conferences and many others. These conferences and summits have a price tag of anywhere from $2,500 to $25,000 a seat! We are there because we're eager to learn.

In fact, we even pay people on our team to read business books. By our subscribing to BetterBookClub.com, new information and knowledge is continuously reinvested directly into our company. How many other companies do you know actually pay their employees to learn by reading books?

When it comes to books, we are insatiable readers. We are always keen to find the next business development, marketing or sales book that we can integrate into the programs we offer for our Client-Partners.

The way Andy always puts it is the company has an unlimited Amazon budget for employees to learn if we're buying a business book or a self-improvement book of some sort. When our employees want to get certified for something, we're there and we'll happily pony up the money for it. We want the smartest people we can get working for us, and that alone makes it worth it to invest as heavily into education as we do.

Some of our favorite books are our own, including *How to Win Clients and Influence People* by Andy Buyting. The second, written by a couple of our teammates Stacey O'Brien and Erika MacLeod, is titled *The Ultimate Culture: It's About DNA, Not Resume*. It's all about our culture here at Tulip Media Group.

Below is a list of other marketing and sales books that we've read that we strongly recommend you pick up:

- *Building a StoryBrand* by Donald Miller
- *Marketing Made Simple* by Donald Miller
- *Exponential Organizations* by Salim Ismail
- The entire *Likeable* series by Dave Kerpen
- *It's Not What You Sell, It's What You Stand For* by Roy Spence
- *To Sell is Human* by Daniel Pink
- *Business Made Simple* by Donald Miller
- *Free the Idea Monkey* by Michael Maddock
- *Ultimate Guide to Google AdWords* by Perry Marshall
- *80/20 Sales and Marketing* by Perry Marshall
- *Marketplace Best Practices* by Tom McFadyen
- *The Average Joe's Marketing Book* by Joe Polish

- *The Ultimate Sales Machine* by Chet Holmes
- *All Marketers are Liars* by Seth Godin
- *Purple Cow* by Seth Godin
- *Storytelling for Startups* by Marc Evans
- *Brand from the Inside* by Libby Sartain
- *The Machine* by Justin Roff-Marsh
- *UnMarketing* by Scott Stratten
- *Secret Service* by John DiJulius III
- *Top of Mind* by John Hall
- *Fusion* by Denise Lee Yohn
- *What Great Brands Do* by Denise Lee Yohn
- *The Challenger Sale* by Matthew Dixon and Brent Adamson
- *The Trust Edge* by David Horsager
- *The New Rules of Sales and Service* by David Meerman Scott
- *Fanocracy* by David Meerman Scott
- *The New Rules of Marketing & PR* by David Meerman Scott
- *Real-Time Marketing & PR* by David Meerman Scott
- *Baseline Selling* by Dave Kurlan
- *Content Inc.* by Joe Pulizzi
- *Branding Is Sex* by Deb Gabor
- *Hooked* by Nir Eyal
- *Fifty Shades of Marketing* by Naresh Vissa
- *No B.S. Marketing to the Affluent* by Dan S. Kennedy
- *No B.S. Direct Marketing* by Dan S. Kennedy
- *The Ultimate Sales Letter* by Dan S. Kennedy
- *Magnetic Marketing* by Dan S. Kennedy
- *Positioning* by Al Ries
- *The Infinite Game* by Simon Sinek
- *Misbehaving* by Richard Thaler
- *Crushing It* by Gary Vaynerchuk
- *Hyper Sales Growth* by Jack Daly
- *The Small Big* by Steve J. Martin, Noah Goldstein and Robert B. Caldini
- *Pricing with Confidence* by Reed K. Holden and Mark R. Burton
- *Storyselling* by Nick Nanton and J. W. Dicks
- *The Automatic Customer* by John Warrillow
- *Blue Ocean Strategy* by Renée Mauborgne and W. Chan Kim
- *Pre-Suasion* by Robert Cialdini
- *On Writing Well* by William Zinsser

- *No Rules* by Reed Hastings and Erin Meyer
- *Steal Like an Artist* by Austin Kleon
- *Backable* by Suneel Gupta
- *Working Backwards* by Colin Bryar and Bill Carr

The reason we share all this with you is to inspire you to take action through education. Learning new skills provides you with a competitive advantage that others cannot take away from you and investing in the knowledge of your team is an excellent way to achieve that.

Additionally, we offer worksheets and courses on the Tulip Media Group website (TulipMediaGroup.com/Tulip-Academy/). There, you have the option to purchase and learn in more detail about SMarketing including pay-per-click advertising, core customer development, content marketing and more.

We would love to hear your feedback on your SMarketing journey and other business development successes.

Good luck!

-       Andy & Jessica

About the Authors

Andy Buyting

Andy's thought leadership journey started when he published his first business book in 2007 and first magazine in 2009. Since that time, he has leveraged his integrated approach to print, digital and interactive marketing strategies to establish himself as a thought leader in marketing and business development.

Through his company; Tulip Media Group, his team empowers others so they can achieve greater business results through an easy and effective marketing strategy. Andy is also a TEDx speaker.

Jessica Embree

Jessica Embree has been the Creative Director at Tulip Media Group for over six years. She is a StoryBrand Certified Guide who works with our Client-Partners to craft their brand identities into compelling stories with clear and consistent marketing messaging. Jessica is also Google Ad Certified and takes the lead on the keyword strategies and research for all of our SMarketing programs.

A lifelong entrepreneur, Jessica started her first business at the age of 10. Under the banner of J&J Blueberry Enterprise, Jessica and her sister, Jennifer, harvested blueberries from their family's blueberry farm and sold them door to door. She was also a competitive fencer and represented her province at the Canada Games.

In her free time, Jessica enjoys speed reading through as many books as she can get her hands on. She is a self-declared bookworm and an avid contributor to Tulip Media's Better Book Club program. Jessica resides on the east coast in New Brunswick with her husband, Evan, and daughter, Emma.